"This is a must read to reawaken our hearts for the little ones in society who are ignored and unheard. There is no room for them. Convicting and compelling, Shank reminds us of Jesus's deep compassion for society's marginalized."

—**Lynn McMillon,** Distinguished Professor of Bible, Oklahoma Christian University, and licensed marriage and family therapist

"Harold Shank writes from the front lines, answering our hopelessness as we face this world's needs. The good news Harold shares in *Listen and Make Room* speaks to my everyday frustration of not knowing what to do and if what I do will even last. This is a book that offers real hope."

—**Emily Y. Lemley,** editor of *Power for Today*

"The way of Jesus seems upside down in our broken world. Listening to and making room for the vulnerable is not the way to get ahead in this life. But Shank demonstrates that this upside-down way of living is, in fact, exactly what this world needs. It is at the heart of the Gospel, and central to the mission of Jesus."

—**Dr. Kent Brantly,** Ebola survivor and coauthor of *Called for Life*

"In *Listen and Make Room*, Dr. Harold Shank brings Scripture to life with poignant, culturally relevant examples. His words will inspire you to change lives, change eternities, and be a servant like Jesus."

—**Sherri Statler,** President of Christian Homes and Family Services

"These extraordinary messages from Harold are shaped by years of his being close to God's heart for the under heard, underserved, and underrepresented. You will hear God's voice as you read this important book."

—**David Jordan,** President and CEO of Agape Child and Family Services in Memphis, Tennessee

"Shank's decades as a minister of the Word shine as he moves easily through texts, weaving a full-bodied understanding of the God who cherishes children, draws them to him, and works on their behalf. Shank's poignant stories remind us that listening and making room for children is God's heart."

—**Holly Catterton Allen,** Professor of Family Studies and Christian Ministries, Lipscomb University

"Harold asks the question, "Do you hear what the children are saying?" It is a question that calls for us to respond like Jesus did. This book is both pastoral and prophetic in tone, with a strong call to action. *Listen and Make Room* is a special book that will rekindle your love for the children in your neighborhoods and living rooms."

—**Scott D. Lambert,** Executive Director of Let's Start Talking

"In his speaking for Network 1:27, Harold's messages consistently focus on our compassion and purpose with children. I am always encouraged and reinvigorated to go and do more for those entrusted to our care. The messages in *Listen and Make Room* are a call to action for each of us as we seek to help the vulnerable in our communities."

—**Nathan Samuel,** President and CEO of Childplace, Inc.

"Harold Shank has been a voice for mercy and justice among Churches of Christ for many years. This book continues that message. It will fill your soul, touch your heart, and on occasion provoke your spirit."

—**Steve Cloer,** preaching minister at Southside Church of Christ, Fort Worth, Texas

"Each chapter of *Listen and Make Room* is deeply rooted in Scripture and filled with invaluable insight, restoration, and hope. This book will bless anyone who loves children, anyone who cares about a broken world, anyone in search of God's solutions to life's most difficult problems, anyone who needs their hope restored."

—**Ken Durham,** Baxter Chair of Preaching in the College of Bible and Ministry, Lipscomb University

"Any time I read or hear something from Harold regarding ministry to children and families, I know it will be an encouraging reminder of why God has called us to this work and of how important caring for orphaned children is to the work of the kingdom!"

—**Chandler Means,** Executive Director of AGAPE of Nashville, Tennessee

"Christians, churches, and organizations seeking to make significant differences in the lives of the people in their communities need to read *Listen and Make Room*. It is breathtaking in its breadth, depth, and its clarion call to attend to the plight of one of the most vulnerable populations in our world. This is a book that can help the kingdom come to earth as it is in heaven."

—**Chris Altrock,** senior preaching minister at Highland Church of Christ in Memphis, Tennessee, and author of *Behind Esther*

"Gripping! Dr. Harold Shank has written another page-turner that shakes you to the core and stirs your compassion. Shank poignantly helps you see that when you listen to what the helpless children are saying, you hear the heartbeat of God. No book has inspired me more than *Listen and Make Room*."

—**James E. Moore,** President of Mount Dora Children's Home, Mount Dora, Florida

"Harold's dynamic storytelling draws together the Word and the readers' thoughts and emotions in a way that inspires mindfulness toward the weak and vulnerable, especially children. He challenges you to see the value of children through the eyes of our Lord."

—**Randy Schow,** Executive Director of Mountain States Children's Home

LISTEN
AND
MAKE
ROOM

JOINING GOD *in* WELCOMING CHILDREN

LISTEN
AND
MAKE
ROOM

HAROLD SHANK

Abilene Christian University Press

LISTEN AND MAKE ROOM
Joining God in Welcoming Children

ACU
PRESS

Copyright © 2020 by Harold Shank

ISBN 978-1-68426-360-8 | LCCN 2019040893

Printed in the United States of America

LIBRARY OF CONGRESS CATALOGING-IN-PUBLICATION DATA
Names: Shank, Harold, author.
Title: Listen and make room : joining God in welcoming children / Harold Shank.
Description: Abilene, Texas : ACU Press, 2020. | Includes bibliographical references.
Identifiers: LCCN 2019040893 | ISBN 9781684263608 (trade paperback)
Subjects: LCSH: Jesus Christ—Example. | Church work with children. |
    Church work with minorities. | Listening—Religious aspects—Christianity.
Classification: LCC BT304.2 .S49 2020 | DDC 259/.22—dc23
LC record available at https://lccn.loc.gov/2019040893

Cover design by Bruce Gore | Gore Studio, Inc.
Interior text design by Sandy Armstrong, Strong Design

For information contact:
Abilene Christian University Press
ACU Box 29138
Abilene, Texas 79699

1-877-816-4455
www.acupressbooks.com

20 21 22 23 24 25 / 7 6 5 4 3 2 1

To four children who remind me to listen and make room:

Carina Antigone Shank

Hannah Ruth Overturf Shank

Amos Oscar Overturf Shank

Mailon Daniel Shank

CONTENTS

PART 4
MAKING ROOM

PART 5
HOPE

LISTEN AND MAKE ROOM

MATTHEW 21:12-17

This book is about listening and making room. It maintains that effective and winsome ministry comes when we hear the cries in the public places and then accommodate the people for whom Jesus made room.

My listening and making-room metaphors depend on a story that appears only in the Gospel of Matthew. It begins with a glorious parade that stretched down the western slopes of the Mount of Olives. Human clothing and tree branches paved the entire road. Jesus, seated on a donkey, led this cheering crowd, and their voices echoed against the city's fortified wall and down its streets.

Jesus was making what is called his triumphal entry into Jerusalem. The whole city seemed stirred by the outbreak of praise. As Jesus sat on the donkey, the vehicle of kings, one of the praises the people shouted was a little-used word from the Old Testament: "Hosanna." Ironically, it is as rarely used today as it was in New Testament times. The word means "save us, I pray." On the wings of the shouted "Hosannas," word spread quickly throughout the city, and talk everywhere was about Jesus.

After reaching the Kidron Valley, Jesus took the path up to the top of Mount Moriah and entered the temple gate. The huge outer court of the temple bustled with commercial activity. Jesus didn't like what he saw, so he took action. He did some housecleaning and cleared out the buyers and moneymakers. Overturning tables and seats, he said to them, "It is written, 'My house shall be called a house of prayer'; but you make it a den of robbers" (Matt. 21:13).

The outer court of the temple had become a shopping center. Jesus knew it had another primary purpose, so he upset the tables and chased out the merchants. Then he quoted Isaiah 56, revealing the purpose of that part of the temple. God meant it for *prayer*. To strengthen his point, he cited Jeremiah 7 and told them they had made it a *den of robbers*. They were doing exactly what their ancestors did in the seventh century BC. So far, this story appears in all four Gospels.

Then this happened: "And the blind and the lame came to him in the temple, and he healed them" (Matt. 21:14).

When Jesus made room, the vulnerable came for prayer. Before his cleansing work on this day, the commercial activities so dominated this temple space that the vulnerable had no means of full access. Now, without having to navigate past the shopkeepers and through the crowds of shoppers, the sightless and those who could not walk sought out Jesus. He treated their ills. He fixed what was broken. He turned the not good back to good. Jesus gave the blind their sight and made the lame walk.

That created room. There was now space for those who had been excluded. These vulnerable and typically unwanted people entered where they had always wanted to be. They found welcome and healing next to Jesus.

I suspect that the next turn of events surprised everybody. The temple court filled with children. The noise of commerce was replaced by the shouts of praise. When the chief priests heard the children, "they were indignant; and they said to him, 'Do you hear what these are saying?' And Jesus said to them, 'Yes; have you never read, "Out of the mouth of babes and sucklings thou hast brought perfect praise"?'" (Matt. 21:15–16).

Only Matthew reports this scene. The story turns to the children gathered around Jesus. After Jesus chased out the shopkeepers and the shoppers, then the lame, the blind, and children had space. In the midst of the huge courtyard, the children flocked to Jesus.

The children shouted, "Hosanna." It's that Hebrew word from Psalm 118. One might translate Psalm 118:25 as "O LORD, Hosanna, we beseech you,

O LORD, send prosperity!" Like the Hebrew word "Hallelujah," it's a word of praise. The word appears only on this occasion in the New Testament.

The children shouted, "Hosanna to the Son of David." Translated, they said, "Save us, O Son of David." It's a statement of faith. The prophets predicted a Messiah who would be the son of David. When Jesus rode in on the donkey, the people shouted numerous lines of praise. One of those lines is the one the children repeated in the temple: "Hosanna to the Son of David." Where did the children learn that line?

- Were the children who praised him in the temple also among the crowds that watched the parade go down the slopes of the Mount of Olives? If so, they heard the word from the adults on the parade route. They just followed the procession into the temple courts.
- Or were the children who shouted Hosanna part of the families of the blind and lame? Had they spent their lives leading their blind uncle or pulling the cart of their lame older sister? When Jesus cleared the temple, they filled up the open space.
- Or were they sent by God to deliver an important message and to create a significant scene? God planned for them to be there to deliver the message, "Hosanna!"

I don't know. I just know that the temple quickly filled with the noise of children.

They shouted, "Hosanna to the Son of David!" Why did they say that? Jesus is about to answer that question.

But before he got to the children's cry, the adults intervened. These adults were the authorities—the ones in charge of holy things. They had the order of worship prepared every week. They sat on the building and grounds committee. They arranged the schedule, controlled the crowds, made the rules, and issued the budgets. That day, they were not happy because they had lost control.

They made an angry demand of Jesus. "**Do you hear what these are saying?**" They meant, "Jesus, do you hear what the children are saying?"

Jesus made his answer quite clear: "Yes."

Do you hear what these are saying, Jesus?

Yes, I hear what these are saying.

Jesus, do you hear what the children are saying?

Yes, I hear what the children are saying.

There's the source of my metaphors. Jesus made room for the vulnerable. He cleared the temple, and it filled with the blind, lame, and children. Then, he listened to those who often have no voice.

Listening and making room.

Author Jonathan Kozol wrote the book *Amazing Grace,* which told about two years he spent in Mott Haven in the Bronx. In the late 1990s, it was one of the poorest, most dangerous, and most unhealthy communities in our country.[1]

He wrote about children. He claimed that the experience of talking to those children was the most important thing he had done as an adult. He painted a remarkable picture of an America that we often don't see:

- He told stories of children being shot.
- He described the apartment fires that left children dead.
- He identified the home of these children as the poorest congressional district in the nation.
- Almost every child had a father or a brother in prison.
- They came from dysfunctional homes.
- They attended schools where none of the restrooms worked.
- These children lived in rat-infested housing projects controlled by drug dealers.

The end of the book has a distressingly long list of children in the Bronx who died while he wrote the volume.

But Kozol insisted he found faith in these children. He built the book around the song *Amazing Grace.* He argued that if grace exists, it's in these children. It was as if these children were shouting "Hosanna to the Son of David."

Kozol found faith in the hearts of these children, but it wasn't the only discovery he made. At one point, the author writes about these children,

---

[1] Jonathan Kozol, *Amazing Grace* (New York: Perennial, 1995).

"They do not yet know that the nation does not love them." The children can see; it's the nation that is blind. "America does not listen to its children."

That's the situation in Matthew 21. Adults, who should have faith, don't. Children, who should be out playing, are the ones who stand for faith. The adults complained, got angry and upset, and seemed preoccupied. The children hung on Jesus's every word, gave praise to God, and shouted statements about deep faith.

The adults, who should have been listening to the children, sought to silence them. They believed faith came from adults, not children. The religious authorities didn't like what the children were doing. They were *indignant*.

"Indignant" appears five times in the New Testament, twice in connection with children. One of those times is here when the religious leaders become angry with the children. The other time is when Jesus was indignant about how the disciples were responding to children in Mark 10. There, Jesus became indignant because his disciples kept the children away.

The religious leaders asked, "Do you hear what the children are saying?" It's a striking question. Are you listening to the children? Jesus, are you listening to these children? Do you hear them?

Jesus answered.

Yes. I hear these children.

I hear their shouting.

I hear what they say.

I'm listening to the children.

Then he elaborated on his affirmation: "Yes; have you never read, 'Out of the mouth of babes and sucklings thou hast brought perfect praise'?" (Matt. 21:16).

After affirming that he heard the children, Jesus quoted Psalm 8:2. It's a poem about God's majesty. The psalm begins by saying we can see God's majesty in nature. Then it says that the same praise of God is found in words of children.

Jesus, in effect, put the question back to the religious leaders. Do YOU hear the children? Are you listening to the children among you? Do you hear this statement of faith?

Children saw what adults refused to see or wouldn't see. The children saw Jesus clear the temple and heal the lame and blind. They responded, "Hosanna to the Son of David."

The adults witnessed Jesus cleanse the same temple, they saw the identical miracles in the courtyard, yet they refused to believe and became angry with the children who did.

Even contemporary commentators try to explain this situation away. Some say this event could not have happened because children were not allowed in the temple. Others say the children are just repeating what their parents said because the children really didn't understand what they were saying. They claim the word "babes" from Psalm 8 doesn't mean "child" but "the weak of the world." They say all this because they don't believe children can have faith.

We're still trying to silence the children.

It's a haunting question:

Do you hear what the children are saying?

It's not a demand to listen to all that all children say. But do you hear what they say about faith? Kozol listened to children in New York City for two years, and he heard faith. He concludes that America does not listen to its children.

I remember the struggle I had as a child. Growing up in an unchurched family, I had no exposure to spiritual training. In my early teens, I started to search for God. I didn't know what to do. I never said anything like Hosanna. I didn't even know the word. I certainly didn't know Jesus.

Then people like Larry Van Steenberg, Ray Beggs, Mildred Stutzman, and others took the time to listen to a child. They really listened. They heard a child seeking faith. They came alongside me and nurtured that calling.

I'd not thought about that part of my life until I read Matthew 21. It was as if Jesus turned to Larry Van Steenberg, Ray Beggs, and Mildred Stutzman and said, "Do you hear what that boy is saying?"

They all said yes.

If they had not listened, I don't know where I'd be today.

This book is a call for us to do the same. In effect, it says we often don't listen to those who have little voice in our world, our culture, and especially in our churches. It says we often fill up all the space ourselves and leave little room for those who have little ability to acquire a spot.

This book is less about doctrine and more about ministry. It may seem at times to be a miscellaneous collection of topics and comments rather than a sustained argument. I'm not as interested in sustaining a thought as I am in sustaining ministry. I've kept the chapters short to keep them accessible. I'm more interested in keeping people on the front line of ministry than in keeping them engaged for two more pages. I'm more focused on inspiration than information.

So you will not find this book heavily footnoted with solid connections between chapters and answers to every objection. I don't engage the systematic and historical thinkers, but rather offer life support for those on the front lines. I seek to call people to join Jesus. Join him in listening to and making room for the blind, the lame, and the children.

People who have a heart for the vulnerable often wear out. This book is based on my experiences with people who consistently listened to children. Each chapter comes from a lesson presented to the leaders of the sixty child care agencies associated with Churches of Christ. They call themselves Network 1:27. These men and women hear the cries of the most rejected and voiceless children in America. They make room for these children in their lives. They seek to provide these children with justice and righteousness.

For over two decades, I gathered with these child care workers as we sought to listen to children and find ways to make room for them in contemporary America. Every year, we meet to compare notes on what we learned and how these children fared. My own role in those gatherings pales in comparison to theirs. They heard the cries of children and other vulnerable people such as the blind and the lame long before I did. In fact, they are the ones who taught me to listen. Kozol's line that "America does not listen to its children" is not entirely true. Good Christian people such as those who are part of the Network 1:27 coalition do listen to the children. They have trained themselves to hear those feeble cries. They see faith where most of us just see noisy children.

They make room for these unwanted children in ways that continue to astound me. They make room for children abandoned by their parents.

They take in the babies whose mothers used drugs, whose fathers don't care, and they give them a home. I'm amazed at what they do. Kozol's line that "They do not yet know that the nation does not love them" may be true of far too many of us, but these good people are on the front lines of making room for the children the rest of us do not want.

These chapters represent over two decades of spending most of a week together every year returning to the core issues of listening and making room. As I looked out every year at those who work with the most troubled children in America, I saw the same faces each time. They became my once-a-year congregation to whom I ministered.

My purpose in being with them was to bring them a word from the Lord. I sought to be a voice from the churches that said, *What you are doing is important.* In another sense, I anticipated telling their stories to the churches with the hope that others would join them in listening and making room.

So, these chapters were not originally written as a book, but they come from short times of encouragement on the front lines of dealing with America's most unwanted. They are like words from the chaplain to the soldiers in the foxholes. Despite their original setting at a conference of those involved with these vulnerable children, they hang together remarkably well. Each had a specific context of which the current reader will be unaware, but the general context is one we all face. They and we live in one of the world's most affluent nations, yet we often fail to hear the cries of the least affluent. They and we live in one of the world's most accommodating countries, yet we often live behind locked doors and make little room for those who have no room of their own.

The chapters do not appear in the chronological order in which they were presented. There's a list at the end of the book that gives that timeline. I've rearranged them into five movements. Given their original context as a chaplain's short word to a frontline soldier, each chapter in a sense covers all five movements. At the end of each chapter, a paragraph called "Continuities" indicates how that particular chapter fits into the overall movement. After that, there are a few questions to invite your own thinking. Here are the five movements:

- **Mission.** At the beginning, eight chapters remind us that in the center of the mission of God are the vulnerable of this world. If we take up God's mission, we will listen and make room. In my judgment, the revival that the contemporary church most needs is found here.
- **Listening to children.** Then I move on to the concerns of the world's most vulnerable people. These vulnerable include children. When we listen to these people through biblically informed eyes, we find the issues that demand our attention. I think we need to spend some time in the public places such as the temple just listening.
- **Listening to God about children.** The Bible contains remarkable instructions about children, especially vulnerable children. God made children, and he keeps on making them. He knows their core needs. Not all of those needs are readily apparent.
- **Making room.** Finding places for those who are left out is the work of discipleship. It's a calling. It's a sacrifice. If we do it out of pity or sentimentality or popularity, we often start and then quit. It's also not just a task we do, but a series of relationships we make. I'm not talking about serving Thanksgiving dinner and then going home. I'm not speaking about finding some inner-city issue, solving it, and then finding a restaurant to feed ourselves. I'm talking about making room in your life for the person you serve. It's about opening a door.

    We tend to think in these categories:

    - us/them
    - safe/dangerous
    - rich/poor
    - disciplined/lazy
    - wise/foolish

Every slash is a closed door that keeps us out of their lives and them out of ours. That / keeps us from them. We are safe. The / keeps us away from the supposedly dangerous. Opening the door takes disciples willing to remove the slash. It affects the way we eat, the way we vote, the places we vacation, and how we spend our money. Listen. Make room.

- **Hope.** Finally, we need regular reminders that encourage us not to give up. One of my mentors told me that most people are looking for hope. Our own hopelessness may make us ignore the cries of the most vulnerable or give up making room because the task seems so overwhelming. We are all looking for some reason to go on. So are the vulnerable of our world. We all need hope.

So read a chapter or two and then go find a child. Take a cup of coffee's worth of this book and then go listen to a person on the edge of life. Then read a few more pages that urge you to make room.

They are crying out in the temple. Do you hear what the children are saying?

WHAT DO YOU THINK?

1. Why did the temple authorities, and so many others, ignore the children?

2. Jesus made room and then listened. The author changes the order to "listen and make room." What do you think of the change?

3. The author suggests there are slashes that keep us separated. What are some of the ways in which we create slashes?

4. What child or vulnerable person do you need to listen to and make room for? How can you begin?

PART 1

MISSION

Jesus was on a mission. Whether it was the day he rode the donkey into Jerusalem, the day he cleansed the temple and listened to the children, or the day he dragged the cross to Golgotha, carried our sins, and died to save us all, he was on the same mission. His mission was rooted in the heart of God.

If we follow Jesus, we take up his mission. If we seek to be like Jesus, we follow him following God. The next chapters explore that mission.

1

IT'S NOT GOOD OUT THERE

GENESIS 1:31

Religious people in Jesus's day kept the lame and blind out of the temple.
But the situation existed long before Jesus's time. Ignoring the cries of faith
from children has a long history. Furthermore, the call to listen and make
room does not first emerge in the outer court of the Jerusalem temple.
The whole mission in front of us has deep roots. I think it takes us back to
the beginning.

Genesis 1 may be one of the world's best-known pieces of literature.
Nearly everybody has heard the line "In the beginning." As it goes on,
there's a rhythm about the Bible's opening chapter. After "In the beginning
God created the heavens and the earth" (Gen. 1:1), God made light.

God said it was **good**.

Then God separated the waters and created dry ground.

God said it was **good**.

Next, he made the plants, grass, trees, and seeds.

They, too, were **good**.

In verse 16, God put the sun, moon, and stars in their places. He looked
at the sky and evaluated his work.

That's **good**.

Then came the sea and sky animals and then the land animals.

Each received the **good** evaluation.

Finally, God created humanity, gave them dominion, and blessed them. In verse 31, he surveyed it all.

It was **very good**.

The rhythm revolves around the word **good**. God made each piece of the world. Then came the evaluation: it was good.

Our world also has a rhythm. But the pulse of our world stands in contrast to the beat of God's new world. Like God, we too make things. However, the things we create fall short of what he made.

We make wars and commit crimes. We look over the resulting death and destruction.

We think it's **not so good**.

Because of inequity, we witness starvation, diseases running rampant, and whole villages without clean water. We look over the pain and suffering and we evaluate.

This situation is **not good**.

Then we hear about the drug epidemic, the sex trade, and corporate dishonesty. We get overwhelmed with the bad decisions and immorality, so we draw our conclusions.

These things are **not good**.

We view the poverty in our cities, the tension between the races, and corruption in government. We shudder at the inequity and inhumanity and think about what we have seen.

This situation **cannot be good**.

We watch a loved one with a terrible disease and call on a friend with cancer. We view their anguish and grief.

Through our tears, we realize it is **not good**.

So, what happened to God's **good** world? Why do we live in such a broken place? Should we forget God's good world? What does the Bible do with the good creation?

Teaching about creation runs throughout the Bible. Twenty-seven of the sixty-six books deal with creation, but it centers in three places:

- First is Genesis 1–2.
- Then there are over forty verses about creation in Psalms.
- Isaiah 40–55 overflows with thinking about creation.

Out of all this writing about creation, the rest of the Bible follows a pattern. A verse cites some issue, and then it says some version of "this is not the way it was at the beginning." Look over this list:

- John knew the world had a high disregard for grace and truth, so he opened his Gospel (John 1) with the reminder that the Word of God existed at the beginning. Grace and truth came by the incarnate Word. In 1 John 1, he said it all happened in the beginning.
- In Athens, Paul saw the world's many man-made gods. But it was not that way in the beginning. Paul reminded them that in the beginning, one God made the world (Acts 17:24).
- The psalmist saw an earth in need of food, life, and renewal. In response, he wrote a song about the way it was at the beginning (Ps. 104:1–25) when God made food, life, and means of renewal.
- Life in Corinth involved the perversion of sexuality. Paul reported it was not so at the beginning. He cited the creation stories to speak of the higher standard of the two becoming one (1 Cor. 6:16).
- People in Jesus's day as well as ours wrestle with divorce. They asked Jesus for clarification. He said, "at the beginning" God set the standard (Matt. 19:4–6).
- Paul spoke of the "dominion of darkness" (Col. 1:13). In that darkness, Paul maintained that the world disregarded human dignity and rejected the way in which the whole world holds together in Christ. He built his case on the created world (Col. 1:15–20).

We see the pattern. Something in our world is broken. The writers of the Bible go back to the beginning. That's not the way it was. That's not the way it's supposed to be. That's not the way God wants it. Keeping creation in mind helps us in two critical ways.

Creation Is Not as It Should Be

Many of us have grown frustrated with the difficulty of sharing our faith. We sense that few people are interested in hearing us talk about our beliefs. Few congregations are growing by winning the lost world. Churches seem more defensive and less on the offense. What's the solution?

Try this plan: Stop people on the street or take a survey on social media. Ask these three questions:

- Are you lost?
- Are you concerned about hell?
- Are you saved?

In the situation that most of us live in, many of the people we ask would view these questions as old-fashioned, out of touch, or irrelevant, and see us as odd, stuck in the past, or a religious fanatic. Even many of the young people in our own churches don't like these questions. For many of us, it's one of the "not goods" of our time.

Then try this plan: Ask the same people, "Do you think the world is broken?" Suddenly, everybody agrees, and we have a conversation. People who go to church and people who don't go to church concur. Folks who do not believe in God and those who have based their entire lives on God have this common ground. Young and old in the same congregation agree. The world is broken.

Creation helps us keep in mind that the world was once good. God made a good world. In fact, it was very good. Our world is filled with "not goods." We should never lose sight of our situation. It becomes the core of why we are here.

Here's the core of our mission. The lines below summarize the biblical challenge. It's the template by which we find our mission. These thoughts wrap up the whole biblical story:

- God made a good world.
- We broke it.
- Jesus came to fix it.
- Those he fixes are asked to join him in restoring his broken world.

God's world was good. We messed it up. But it is not so messed up that it can't be fixed. In fact, that's why Jesus came. He started a movement to fix it. We join him in that mission of restoring the broken world.

Once we see this template in its broad parameters, we begin to see it everywhere. Put that template over some key passages.

Try Jesus's programmatic statement in Luke 4:18–19:

The Spirit of the Lord is upon me, because he has anointed me
to preach good news to the poor. He has sent me to proclaim
release to the captives and recovering of sight to the blind, to set
at liberty those who are oppressed, to proclaim the acceptable
year of the Lord.

It was a good world, and the good news is that it can be good again, because
Jesus came to fix it. Then he lists some of those he planned to fix. Read on
in Luke as he calls those he heals to join his crusade.

Put the template over James 1:27:

Religion that is pure and undefiled before God and the Father is
this: to visit orphans and widows in their affliction, and to keep
oneself unstained from the world.

There was a good world out there that was pure and undefiled. God wants
to restore it. So he calls us who seek to be cleaned from this world's blots
to fix the situation of those still broken. The most crucial examples of the
broken are the orphans and widows.

Think about the template and the judgment scene in Matthew 25. It's
like a video of the Judgment Day. God divides humanity into those who
will live with him and those who will not. A few seek an explanation. "Why
did we make it into heaven?" Jesus responds, "Don't you know? You fed me,
gave me something to drink, provided clothing, visited me in prison, and
tended me when I was sick." The saved ask, "When did we do that, Jesus?"
Here's what they hear Jesus say: "When you listened and made room for
the least in this world, you did it to me." Others don't understand why they
did not make it. Jesus said, "I fixed you, and you didn't help fix others." It's
the same template about fixing the broken world.

It's a return to the very good world of God in Genesis 1. Who are those
allowed in? It is those who took time to fix the broken, the hungry, the
thirsty, the sick, and the imprisoned. He says that when you pay attention
to fixing the broken things, you are paying attention to him.

God's mission of restoring the good creation, of fixing the broken
world, keeps us in contact with the real world around us. God's mission
pulls us out of our suburban isolation, our wealthy cocoons, our protective

investment accounts, and brings us face-to-face with the broken. Everybody thinks the world is broken. It's the common ground between people with no faith and those with faith.

God's Mission: Restore Our Broken World

Trying to fix the broken world on our own discourages us before we ever start and dooms us to failure if we try. But facing the brokenness of the world means remembering the power of God.

The Bible keeps repeating the creation story (especially in Genesis, Psalms, and Isaiah) because it is the greatest evidence of God's power. He put all this stuff here. He made it. He set it in motion. If he made it, can't he fix it when it's broken? That's why the rest of the biblical writers who find something broken say, "It wasn't this way at the beginning. Let's restore it like it was."

We tend to adopt the pessimistic views of those around us that some things are just broken. It's not worth fixing them. It's just better to not listen and refuse to make room. Our pessimism tends to drive us to say, "Let's go to church, shut the doors, and sing loud enough to drown out the cries of the vulnerable. Make sure we keep the doors locked so the unwanted can't come in."

We have to decide who we believe. Remember the nursery rhyme about Humpty Dumpty? It has roots in eighteenth-century England. It has four lines:

Humpty Dumpty sat on a wall.
Humpty Dumpty had a great fall.
All the king's horses and all the king's men
Couldn't put Humpty together again.

Too many people believe Humpty Dumpty over Genesis 1. We think the world is too broken to fix. We think if all the king's men couldn't do it, how can God fix it? Why listen to the children if they are beyond repair? There are not enough hospitals to fix all the broken eggs. So we listen to Humpty Dumpty over God.

Creation reminds us that God, not the king or his horses, made the good world.

I knew a man named Jacob. He got so angry at church that he walked out and never returned. He wouldn't let his family go to church. He kept his two boys from learning about God. He turned his anger on his wife and sons. He filled the home with malice, deceit, and strife. He fought with his son. He took his son's wages and spent the money. He fought with everybody. He created such a broken home that at age twelve, his oldest son left home.

In all my years in ministry, I don't know if I witnessed a home with more dysfunction. The anger seemed too deep to heal—a home that was just beyond repair. As I think back on my own views of this family, I realize I became a follower of the Humpty Dumpty rhyme. This family seemed beyond the ability of either the king's men or God to repair it.

Now I believe.

The man named Jacob who left church mad and created a home filled with malice, deceit, and strife was my grandfather. The twelve-year-old boy who ran away from home was my father. Then, I entered the picture. But I testify to you that I witnessed God intervene in this family and fix much of our broken family. I am forever grateful to a God who fixed what was broken.

I'm not sure what your family faces. It may be sexual deviation, or disobedience, or deceit. I do know what your neighborhood and city faces. Down the street from where you live are houses filled with broken people. People bent, bruised, and broken by life walk the streets of every city. We find people around us practicing and suffering from every one of the sins in those lists found in the New Testament. It's almost overwhelming. Even if we had all the king's horses and all the king's men, we couldn't restore this Humpty to his original good state.

But there is not a single person or a single sin or a single problem beyond the power of God in Jesus Christ.

I'm not sure what you will face when you start to listen and open the door to make some room. It may be alcoholism, atheism, and anarchism. It may make you think like Humpty Dumpty.

Go back to creation. Go back to the way things were meant to be. Our world is broken. Our thinking is broken. Too often, we either ignore what is happening around us or we think it can't be fixed. We've grown so used to the broken boxes in which we live that we are blind to the potential God has in mind. We see weaknesses; God sees strengths. We see what little we can do; God sees what remains to be done. I see my little patch of geography; God sees the world. I see limits; God does the impossible.

God created the world. He made it good. We broke it. He offers to fix it and asks us to help.

When it's all repaired, we'll hear him say:

"That's good."

Continuities. Listening and making room comes in the broader context of God's mission to the world. Vulnerable children are part of our world's "not good." Our listening and making room is one way we join Jesus in fixing the broken world.

WHAT DO YOU THINK?

1. What "not goods" do you see in your world?

2. Give an example of Humpty Dumpty thinking.

3. How does the Christian worldview (God created a good world, we broke it, Jesus fixed it, and he asks us to join him) differ from other dominant worldviews?

4. The author shares an example of the brokenness in his family and God fixing it. Share an example you are familiar with concerning God fixing a broken person or family.

2

DON'T LOSE SIGHT OF JESUS

HEBREWS 12:12

There's another version of "it's a not-good world" that we see in many movies and television shows. There's a moment when somebody has been wounded or injured. It might be a battlefield casualty or a drug-deal-gone-bad shooting or a terrible car accident. In every case, the first responder arrives at the side of the injured person. In most instances, and there are few exceptions, the first responders say the same thing. They look over the injury, they survey the scene, they tear off the clothing, and they take a pulse. Then invariably they say:

"It's okay. You're going to be okay."

I understand that we want to think the best. We need to treat people in shock. If there's not some chance of success, then why try? Yet in the movies and the prime-time shows in most cases, it's not okay. Their pain increases. Medical people are far away. Nothing can be done.

Lewis Smedes tells of flying from Los Angeles to Michigan to spend a few days with a friend dying of cancer.[1] The two men had been roommates. They'd shared thirty years of friendship. Smedes wanted to visit his friend when he still had strength to talk. When it came time to leave, Smedes walked away from the hospital bed, stopped at the door, and looked back at

---

[1] Lewis Smedes, *How Can It Be All Right When Everything Is All Wrong?* (San Francisco: Harper and Row, 1982), 13.

his friend. The sick man lifted his head, smiled, and said, "It's all right." As Smedes left the hospital, all he could think about was that it wasn't all right.

"It's not okay" describes the state of our lives and our world. Even though we say, "It's okay," it's not.

- The bills come in and we have no money to pay them.
- There's been no raise in five years.
- Murder rates are up and their locale draws closer to where we live.
- Children still die every day from preventable causes.
- There are more unwanted children than there are foster parents, house parents, or adoptive parents.
- It's not okay.

The people who first received the New Testament book of Hebrews in the mail lived in the same "it's not okay" world. The author of Hebrews talks about their hard struggle and exposure to public abuse and affliction (Heb. 10:32–33). They had not yet had to shed their own blood (Heb. 12:4), but some of their number were in prison, facing ill-treatment (Heb. 13:3). Their challenge was to remember them and bear abuse as Jesus had endured—"outside the gate in order to sanctify the people" (Heb. 13:12–13).

The author of Hebrews goes on to note they had responded to this "it's not okay" world in one of three ways:

- They drifted away from their faith (Heb. 2:1–4). They gave up on God.
- They allowed themselves to be deceived about reality (Heb. 3:13). They pretended the world was not broken.
- They became disobedient to what God wanted them to do (Heb. 4:11). They knew they could make a difference, but they didn't try.

In light of all this "it's not okay" world, the writer then makes this remarkable challenge:

Therefore lift your drooping hands and strengthen your weak knees, and make straight paths for your feet, so that what is lame may not be put out of joint but rather be healed. (Heb. 12:12–13)

It's easy to see it as a "grin-and-bear-it passage." Put on your pants and get to work. No pain, no gain.

The conclusion from Hebrews 12:12–13 raises questions: How can we lift drooping hands when we know the world is not okay? How can we have strong knees when it's not all right? How can we walk straight in a crooked world?

The book of Hebrews responds by telling us one crucial fact. Our "it's not okay" world and all its potentially harmful situations can be overcome by one unique person and his mission. The author of Hebrews offers one antidote to cure the illnesses. He provides one source of brightness to light the way. He gives one standard to emerge as the final authority. Those wavering or manipulated or outright rebellious meet their match in this one person.

His name is Jesus.

Hebrews 1–2 (more on this section in the next chapter) gives one grand presentation of Jesus. He is wonderful. He is God supreme. But despite his grandness, he saves me, keeps me, and delivers me. The book's opening verses remind us that God speaks through Jesus, who created the world and reflects God's glory. He upholds our whole existence by his word. He arranged for our lives to be purified of their impurities. Now he sits next to Majesty, with authority over the angels and a name far superior to theirs. That's Jesus.

How does Jesus help us when all we can see and think is "it's not okay"? Hebrews lingers over three thoughts that comprise the heart of our mission to fix a broken world. Here, we find our marching orders to listen and make room.

Never Lose Sight of Jesus

Hebrews calls him our trailblazer or our pioneer. Jesus looked the "not okay" world in the face and triumphed. Jesus experienced all the "it's not right" stuff that we do, but he overcame. If we take up his mission, we must never take our eyes off Jesus. No matter what happens, it will be okay.

In the 1982 television miniseries *Niccolo Paganini*, the Czech actor Vlastimil Harapes plays the role of the nineteenth-century Italian violinist. After performing several pieces, he turned to one of his favorites, a violin concerto. As he played to an attentive audience, one of the strings on his violin snapped and fell useless at the side of his instrument. He continued to play, relying on his skill to improvise and play on three strings. Then, another string snapped. Now with two strings rendered useless, Paganini continued to play the concerto on the two remaining strings. As he neared the end, a third string broke. The concert violinist finished the piece with one string.

Jesus created the world, sat at the right hand of God, and then came to the earth. Friends deserted him. One string broke. The crowds thinned. String number two fell to the side. They nailed him to the cross. String number three snapped. But he played his music to the end.

Sometimes life forces us to use one string. Hebrews affirms that we can count on that happening. The world is broken. But we do not quit playing. Don't ever give up on Jesus.

Never Lose Sight of Our Christian Friends

One of the great lines in the book is Hebrews 3:13: "Exhort one another every day, as long as it is called 'today,' that none of you may be hardened by the deceitfulness of sin." Later, the writer urges, "Let us consider how to stir up one another to love and good works, not neglecting to meet together" (Heb. 10:24–25).

As we pursue the mission of Jesus, as we join God in fixing the broken world, as we listen and make room, we do not do it alone. It's not all up to you or me. We join hands with others who follow the one who came to fix it all.

The Institute for the Arts in Washington, DC, had two pieces of art on display. One, entitled *Friends* by Mark Weber, depicts a disheveled man with uncombed hair and furrowed brow, obviously in need of help. On his shoulders are two strong hands representing his friends. The other is a small bronze statue entitled *The Boost* by Lee Richardson. A kneeling mother holds her child toward heaven. The statue has the child's hands reaching even higher.

Both artists convey the point of Hebrews. We need each other. We are not alone. Our fellowship with each other as God's daughters and sons gives us a boost in a "not okay" world. We need each other to confront the "not goods" and make them into "goods." We listen and make room together.

Never Underestimate the Power of Faith

Hebrews 11 lists a group of people who faced a "not okay" world, and who did so triumphantly through their faith. Each person on the list knew about struggle, pain, difficulty, and the bitterness of life. They experienced our world but finished ahead of us. Their bodies were covered with sweat, their legs tired, their faces drawn, but there they stand, cheering us on. They ran the race by faith.

John G. Paton worked on the South Sea islands translating the Bible into the language of a primitive tribe.[2] While translating the Gospel of John, he realized that the local language had no word for faith. About that time, a local chief, whom he had befriended, came to his house exhausted. He put two chairs together and used them as a bed. He told Paton he could put his full weight on those chairs. The chief used one word for the phrase "put his whole weight on." Paton realized he had found a word for faith. When the world overflows with the "not good," we can put all our weight on God.

When it's not right, and we're on a mission for God through Jesus Christ, Hebrews points to a way out. When there seem to be more "not goods" than "goods," when there are too many children and not enough room, we need to hear the word that the people in Hebrews got in the mail: "Lift your drooping hands and strengthen your weak knees." There's work to be done.

Continuities. This chapter and the next one take up the thought of Hebrews. The letter addressed a group of Christians who forgot their mission. The writer directs them back to Jesus. It seems to be a simple lesson, but it's often exactly what we need to hear as individuals or churches to get back on track.

---

[2] Cited in Christopher Shennan, *The Making of a Personal Evangelist: Winning the World for Christ—One by One* (Morrisville: Lulu Publishing, 2014), 122–23.

WHAT DO YOU THINK?

1. Think of times when everybody said, "It's okay," but you knew it was not okay.

2. Why did the writer of Hebrews need to remind his readers to rely on Jesus?

3. Of the three significant messages from Hebrews, which do you most need to hear?

4. The recipients of Hebrews responded to the "it's not okay" world by drifting, being deceived, and disobedience. Are people responding this way today? Explain.

3

WONDERFUL, WONDERFUL, JESUS IS TO ME

HEBREWS 1:1-4

My friend David sent his son Jerome to a Christian college. (I've changed some names to protect his identity, but it's a true sad tale.) Jerome did well there and then continued on to graduate school, where he received his doctorate. After he received his final degree, the Christian school invited him back to join the faculty. A few years into his tenure there, he announced he was an atheist. He left to teach at a state university. Distraught, David asked me what he could do.

I remember not knowing what to say.

One Sunday after I preached at a church outside Wheeling, West Virginia, a middle-aged woman pulled me aside. She told me the story of her teenage daughter. With great pain, she revealed the girl had moved in with her boyfriend, started doing drugs, and experimented with alcohol. All of it created a wall of bitterness between them. She asked me, "What should I do?"

I clearly remember thinking that I'm not at all sure what to tell her.

We've all been there. We knew somebody who drifted away, a person with a friend who gets deceived and friends can't persuade them otherwise. Someone in the family directly disobeys the core commands of God. We visit with a homeless man with the "will work for food" sign. We watch a video about children dying in some faraway country. We listen and then don't know how to make room.

We wonder: What do we do? How do we respond?

To a church where the people were drifting away (Heb. 2:1), giving in to deception (3:13), and where some were overtly disobedient (3:19), the writer's response is direct: God sent you Jesus. The opening words of Hebrews 1:1–4 offer a tenfold description of Jesus filled with superlative roles, verbs, and phrases:

- God spoke through his Son.
- Jesus is heir of all things.
- Jesus created the world.
- Jesus reflects the glory of God.
- Jesus is stamped with the likeness of God's nature.
- Jesus upholds the universe by the word of his power.
- Jesus made purification for sins.
- Jesus sits at the right hand of Majesty on high.
- Jesus is superior to the angels.
- Jesus's name is more excellent than that of the angels.

Then, the author cites eight Old Testament passages filled with superlative verbs and phrases.

- In Psalm 2, God says, "You are my son."
- God says in 2 Samuel 7, "I am his father, he is my son."
- Psalm 89 has God claiming "He is my firstborn."
- Psalm 97 reports that angels worship him.
- Psalm 104 states that he is above the angels.
- Psalm 45 tells us the Son lives forever.
- Psalm 102 reveals that the Son stays the same forever.
- Psalm 110 concludes that the Son sits at the right hand of God.

Hebrews chapter 2 continues to talk about Jesus. The one greater than the angels moves into our neighborhood. The one who created the earth now visits the earth. The one above suffering comes to suffer. The one who created life comes to die.

Hebrews 1 and 2 tell the whole story of Jesus. He's the leader of our mission. He turns the not good into good. He came to fix the broken world.

After he fixes us, he calls us to join him in tending to others. We are to listen and make room. But the mission revolves around Jesus.

Hebrews 1	Hebrews 2
Above the angels	Lower than the angels
Transcendent	Immanent
Creator	Savior

These first two chapters of Hebrews are summarized by the old song *Wonderful, Wonderful,* written by Haldor Lillenas in 1930.

> Wonderful, wonderful, Jesus is to me
> Counselor, Prince of peace, mighty God is He
> Saving me, keeping me, from all sin and shame
> Wonderful is my redeemer, praise His name!

In Hebrews 1, Jesus is wonderful, counselor, and Prince of peace. He's the mighty God. In Hebrews 2, Jesus saves me. He keeps me from all my sin and shame.

The writer to the Hebrews aims to show how their situation is countered by Jesus. How can you drift away when God sent you the most excellent one he could send? How can you be deceived by cheap imitations when God sent you the real thing? How can you disobey when God gave you his best? So how does this perspective help us as we respond to the drifting, the deceived, and the disobedient? Hebrews 1 and 2 help us in three ways:

Remember God Gave Us the Best

The cross was not purchased from a discount lumber store. Jesus didn't lead a ho-hum life. God did not send a low-ranking angel. We are not told, "Follow Moses; he's a good choice." God sent the best. God chose the excellent. The blood shed at the cross was not donated by the Red Cross; it was divine plasma that cost God his life. God didn't send a sheep from his pasture, but the only son from his house.

Hebrews 1 and 2 remind us he is the best of all, excellent, above the angels, perfect, sits at the right hand of God. Jesus is the best.

Remember There Are No Better Options

There is no book you can write, no office you can hold, no goal you can reach, no place you can live, no degree you can get, no person you can know, no stardom you can achieve, no position you can play on any team, no instrument you can master, no music you can learn, no place you can travel, no corner office you can attain, no amount of money you can possess, no kind of car you can drive, no brand of clothing you can wear, no pleasure you can experience, no house you can build that will satisfy your deepest, most profound longing better than knowing Jesus Christ.

He created your job, your mate, your children, and your home. He created the longings you have, the desires you feel, the purpose you need, the goals you see, and the fulfillment you want. There are no better options.

Remember the Tremendous Cost

Hebrews presses the theme: Jesus died once for all. God himself took our place. It wasn't the backup quarterback or a temporary employee or a last-minute substitute. He was number one. He came himself. The best, the most excellent, the Creator, the one above all angels—that one took our place.

Perhaps we drift because in drifting we hope to chance on something better. Perhaps we believe what the deceivers say because we sense that God held back. Perhaps we disobey to find out how far he will go to get us back. When all is said and done, there is nothing better. Nobody could be more truthful, and there's nothing he's not already done that he could do to give your life meaning and purpose.

During the last days of communism, several of us went to Kiev, Ukraine, to follow up on the Herald of Truth religious television programs that we had put on the superstation in the Ukrainian capital. Over a thousand people attended our follow-up events. One night, I met two teenage boys.

They invited me to the underground church they attended in rural Ukraine. They had a small hut hidden in the woods where they met to sing and praise God. It looked like a gingerbread house, with several different kinds of building materials used in its construction. The backless wooden benches offered no comfort. They covered them with brown wrapping paper to provide some protection from the raw splinters. Three bare light bulbs lit the room.

The two teenage boys who invited me went to that church against the wishes of their parents. Five older women sat at the front. One cried during the whole service. Their husbands forbade them to go to church. A middle-aged physician sat at the back with his two sons. His atheist wife opposed his churchgoing.

I talked with the worshippers. One said, "My mother is a communist, but she's starting to come to church." Another noted, "We don't have enough to eat, but with Jesus, things are looking up." A third reported, "I have cancer because of the nuclear disaster at Chernobyl, but Jesus has saved my soul."

I've often thought about that church in the woods. What kept them from drifting away? Why did they not believe all the deceivers around them? Why not disobey God to get ahead now? The answer: they knew the truth of Hebrews and the King of glory, Jesus himself.

Continuities. The book of Hebrews gives us the theological groundwork for how Jesus keeps us on mission. With that in mind, we now turn to how Jesus himself conceived his purpose.

WHAT DO YOU THINK?

1. What other songs about Jesus reflect the themes in Hebrews?

2. Why did the readers of Hebrews need to be reminded about the importance of Jesus? Do we need that reminder?

3. Why do Christians like the ones in the Ukrainian underground church risk so much to follow Jesus?

4. Do you know Christians suffering in difficult situations that have not drifted, been deceived, or disobeyed? Share their stories.

4

OUR FATHER'S PASSION

LUKE 4:16-30

One day when I lived in Memphis, the metropolitan newspaper printed a small article, buried somewhere near the back of the paper. In less than fifty words, it reported that police had found the unidentified body of a woman floating in the Mississippi River. A follow-up article a few days later identified her as Deborah Lois Wright, a mentally ill woman who lived on the streets.

Someone familiar with the situation told me that they buried her in the county cemetery in one of the lots donated for the homeless. Nine people came to her funeral. Several were caseworkers from the Department of Human Services, two were inner-city ministers, and the others were from the funeral home. Next to the casket was one vase of flowers. That was it. A life was lived, and people who knew her sent one spray of flowers.

At times, the world seems hopeless. It's easy to give up or think that it won't get any better. There are too many children and not enough room. There are too many "not goods" and not enough "goods." There are too many "it's not okays."

But it also makes us wonder. Why is the world this way? Who is supposed to take care of people like Deborah Lois Wright? Where is God in all these questions? It leads me back to Jesus.

Luke 4 provides us with a good place to start. This passage details a critical, central, defining moment for Jesus that goes to the core of who he is and what he came to do. If we are going to be like him, this is a good place to investigate his face. If we are going to be the body, this passage is a perfect place to find our head. If we want to walk in his steps, here is the starting line.

Jesus had been in Judea fasting and praying in the wilderness somewhere east of Jerusalem. He faced three temptations from Satan, never succumbed, and triumphed over evil. Then he returned to Galilee to preach and stopped by his hometown synagogue. They asked him to read. He took the scroll of the prophet Isaiah. Scrolls of this prophet were about twenty-five feet long, but Jesus opened to the spot that he wanted to read. We pick up the story from Luke 4:18–19:

> The Spirit of the Lord is upon me, because he has anointed me
> to preach good news to the poor. He has sent me to proclaim
> release to the captives and recovering of sight to the blind, to set
> at liberty those who are oppressed, to proclaim the acceptable
> year of the Lord.

He put the scroll away and turned to the gathered crowd and told them that that passage had been fulfilled that day in their hearing.

In effect, Jesus announced his mission: preach good news to the poor. His life would focus on the poor, the captives, the oppressed, and the brokenhearted. In a world before formal mission statements, Jesus succinctly stated his purpose.

The next chapters of Luke follow Jesus as he plays out that mission. As I read the material, what happens next refers back to his mission:

- Six times in the next few chapters, Jesus preached good news.
- Six times, he reached out to the hurting and vulnerable.
- Three times, he prayed.
- Six times, he discipled his followers.
- Six times, he encountered resistance.

In all of it, he stayed on mission. He preached good news to the poor.

After Jesus announced his mission, the hometown folks became angry. He pointed out that most insiders turned away from God's power and that ministry finds success in the most unexpected places, like Elijah's work with a foreign widow and Elisha with a Syrian general.

All this information raises a critical question. Why does Jesus come to preach good news to the poor? Why does he minister to the down-and-out? Why does Jesus become known for how he treats the world's most vulnerable people?

Jesus answered those questions. When he opened the Isaiah scroll, he read from Isaiah 61. The context for the passage in Isaiah 61 comes earlier. In Isaiah 56, the prophet called for a world of "righteousness and justice." Christopher Wright says the best translation of those two words into English is "social justice."[1] In Isaiah 58, the prophet spoke of ministry to the hungry, poor, and desperate. In Isaiah 61, the prophet announced that God's Spirit will send a person to preach good news to the poor. That's the line that Jesus read and took as his mission statement.

So why does Jesus set good news to the poor as his mission? He got it from Isaiah.

All of that raises another question. Why does Isaiah call for preaching good news to the poor? Strikingly, both Jesus and Isaiah build on the book of Deuteronomy. Jesus quoted from the book of Deuteronomy three times in his spiritual war with Satan in the Judean wilderness just before arriving in Nazareth.

Deuteronomy records three sermons by Moses on the eve of the conquest of the Promised Land. He gave them a vision and called for establishing an ideal community. It was to be a nation that loved God and loved its neighbor. Read Deuteronomy 30:19–20:

> I call heaven and earth to witness against you this day, that I have set before you life and death, blessing and curse; therefore choose life, that you and your descendants may live, loving the LORD your God, obeying his voice, and cleaving to him; for that means life to you and length of days, that you may dwell in the land which the LORD swore to your fathers, to Abraham, to Isaac, and to Jacob, to give them.

---

[1] Christopher Wright, *Old Testament Ethics for the People of God* (Downers Grove, IL: IVP Academic, 2004), 257.

God wanted Israel to have life, blessing, peace, and love. God called for a community that looked after the vulnerable, paid attention to the disenfranchised, and brought the year of the LORD's favor to the poor. We will dig deeper into this point in Chapter Seven.

So, when Jesus mounted the pulpit in the Nazareth synagogue, he chose a text that captured the heart of God and reflected the core of Scripture. God made a good world, but we broke it. God tried in many ways to send people to patch it up and to fix our mistakes. Finally, Jesus came with the ultimate sacrifice that repaired all our core brokenness. Then he called those he fixed to join him in reaching out to others who are broken. He sent us out to listen and make room.

Why did Jesus preach good news to the poor? Why did he call that his mission? It came directly from the Father. *It is the core of God's heart.* The mission to listen and make room ultimately comes from God.

While I lived in Memphis, we sponsored a school store where children and their families who could not otherwise afford school supplies could come and shop in a respectful and grace-filled environment. One year, a grandmother came with her grandchildren. Afterward, she wrote a kind note thanking us. Then she said that she lived in a public housing project and asked if we would come and teach the children about Jesus.

A couple of weeks later, we started a class for children in the community center of that housing project. Several months later, adults began to come to learn about Jesus. Then they asked, "Why can't we be a church?" So, they began to meet on Sunday morning, and they called themselves the Downtown Church of Christ. They ministered to the poor and the homeless, even the mentally ill ones.

Then four years later, the police found a woman's body floating on the Mississippi River. Four days later, there was a funeral. There was only one spray of flowers at the funeral for Deborah Lois Wright.

The card read:

"To our sister Deborah.

From your brothers and sisters at the Downtown Church of Christ."

Preach good news to the poor. It's from the heart of God.

> **Continuities.** Taking life just one piece at a time often brings it into focus. That's what we get in Luke 4. Jesus used the synagogue reading to state his mission. The story of one vulnerable woman who met an untimely end takes a "not good" and shows how God made it into a "good."

WHAT DO YOU THINK?

1. How does Jesus's statement in Luke 4 differ from other mission statements you know?

2. What other passages point to God's concern for the vulnerable?

3. What reaction do you have to the Deborah Lois Wright story? What details are missing?

4. Write out your personal mission statement. Jesus lived his mission. How are you living yours?

5

LISTEN TO THE HEARTBEAT

LUKE 15:11-24

Richard Dawkins, the British evolutionary biologist, former professor at Oxford, wrote *The God Delusion* in 2006, which even years later is still widely quoted. The dust jacket says, "*The God Delusion* makes a compelling case that belief in God is not just wrong but potentially deadly." In the book, Dawkins claims, "The God of the Old Testament is arguably the most unpleasant character in all fiction."[1]

We don't have to be atheists like Dawkins to wonder about the same issues. What is God like? Is he there? Is he as bad as Dawkins makes him out?

God calls us to take up his mission to listen and make room. Is that the mission we want to follow? If people like Dawkins are tossing him out, is it good for us to build our lives around him? Is Dawkins right? Is spending our lives following God just another "not good" and "not okay"?

Perhaps no verse in the Bible tells me more about God than Luke 15:20: "And he arose and came to his father. But while he was yet at a distance, his father saw him and had compassion, and ran and embraced him and kissed him." The line comes in the middle of what's most often called the parable of the prodigal son. The younger of two sons asked his father for his share of the inheritance. He took the money, left home, got involved

---

[1] Richard Dawkins, *The God Delusion* (Boston: Houghton Mifflin Harcourt, 2006), 31.

in wild living with immoral friends, fell into poverty, came to his senses, wrote a speech to give to his father, and headed home. As he approached the family farm, he saw his father waiting for him at the gate. The father ran, greeted his lost son, and welcomed him home.

- The characters in the parable represent us and our world.
- Some of us are the runaway son wanting to come home.
- Others are the smug older brother who thinks he's better than the lost son.
- The father represents the heart of God and those who seek his mission.

The problem is many people just catch a fleeting glimpse of God. They draw quick conclusions. They read stories like the one in 1 Samuel 15:3 where God orders Saul to kill all the men, women, and children. Without any investigation of the horrible wrong that God's instructions address, we simply conclude, "I could not serve a God like that." We look at the evil in our world and easily say, "I can't believe in a God who allows that to happen." Rather than explore the significance of why those events go unchecked, we check out.

The Bible offers a remarkable number of in-depth portraits of God. In Exodus 34:5–7, God provides the longest self-portrait of the divine being in Scripture. Jesus hanging on the cross to right all the world's wrongs gives a drastically alternative view of God. But that one verse in the prodigal son parable tells us something vitally important about God.

Charles Dickens's novel *Martin Chuzzlewit* tells the story of old Martin and his young grandson of the same name. Old Martin is rich; young Martin rebellious. The boy leaves his grandfather's care to become an architect's apprentice. Done with that, he becomes a vagrant, then a world traveler, then an investor, later a pioneer. Young Martin ends up in a swamp on the American frontier.

Young Martin finds his situation hideous. He sees his failures, so he decides to go home. On the way, he writes a speech to give to his grandfather Martin. "I come to ask your forgiveness, not so much in hope for the future, but in regret for the past. All I want is a job."

Old Martin looks at his wayward grandson and rejects his offer.[2]

It's pretty clear what Dickens is doing. He retells the old parable of the prodigal son, but Dickens writes the ending we expect. We don't expect the father at the gate. The God Dawkins describes in *The God Delusion* would never be there. The God who allows bad things to happen would not welcome home the wayward son. He would not listen. He would not make room. He would not fix what was broken.

Dickens's portrait of God matches Dawkins's negative description of God. Our quick conclusions about God expect him to tell the younger son, "Go sleep on the street. I hope you've learned your lesson. After what you did, don't come around here again."

I remember a friend telling a story about a family reunion when he was eight. With the extended family gathered around the picnic table, he spilled his drink. His father reached across the picnic table, in front of all the relatives, and smacked the little boy across his face. The man said that slap was a crucial event in his life.

It's old Martin all over again. It's Dawkins's old, raging, bitter god. He's not a god worth following. But there's more to the story.

Kenneth Bailey lived in the Middle East for many years. He argues that we must read the parable of the prodigal son against the background of village life. Urbanites can't understand the story in the same way as rural folks. He makes two quick points:[3]

First, when the younger son left, he offended the whole village; and when he returned, Bailey says he faced hostility throughout the neighborhood. Boys would throw stones. Adults looked at him with anger. Most refused to speak to him. No wonder he waited so long to come home.

Second, adult men in ancient villages didn't run. Running while wearing a flowing robe could be a humiliating experience. Most cultures do not expect to see great men running in public. Yet this father ran to meet his son.

That background sets the stage for the father dealing with the lost son. A man in rags approached the village. The neighbors recognized him as

---

[2] Charles Dickens, *Martin Chuzzlewit* (London: Chapman & Hall, 1843).
[3] Kenneth E. Bailey, *Poet & Peasant and Through Peasant Eyes* (Grand Rapids: William B. Eerdmans, 1976), 161–62, 178, 181.

the boy next door who ran away with the family fortune. They quickly surmised from his appearance that he'd lost the father's money. It wasn't just the father's money; it was their common wealth. They had fewer assets because of this no-good son. They were not going to listen to him. Nobody wanted to make room. News spread through the village. Hostile and angry people came to look. A few shoved him around.

Then the door opened. Out came one of the most respected men in the village. He ran past the old women, through the crowd of children. He stirred up dust on the unpaved road and pushed the mob aside. His robes flowed in the wind. He would not be stopped. Despite what the world said and what the villagers thought, he ran and took his son in his arms.

We assume the boy will bow before the father, but he can't because his father's embrace keeps him erect. The son didn't expect this reaction. He'd prepared to run the gauntlet, but his father faced the mob and ran the gauntlet for him.

In quick succession, the father called for his most precious possessions:

- Go to my closet and get my best robe, the one for special occasions, the one I wore to my wedding. Put that robe on my son.
- Then bring the ring, the one I use to seal business transactions. Get the one that reflects my position and my responsibility.
- Also, bring the sandals. I know servants go barefoot. I know the field hands don't wear foot coverings. I want my son to have the best.
- Then he sent a servant to prepare a feast with a fatted calf. One calf would feed nearly a hundred people. Meat spoiled in this world if not eaten on the day of its slaughter. The villagers realized they had just been invited to a banquet.

This father is not the god Dawkins describes. He's the God of Scripture. He's the God who made a very good world. He's a God who fixes the broken. He's a God who listens. He's a God who makes room. He's a God who sends the very best.

The beloved hymn *Amazing Grace* by John Newton draws on the Luke 15 story of the prodigal son. While at sea in 1748, the ship Newton was on encountered a terrific storm. Like the returning son, Newton called out for mercy. The ship reached shore. Soon, he became a preacher, advocated for the end of the slave trade, and wrote hymns.

The line from the hymn, "I once was lost, but now I'm found," not only reflected the story in Luke 15 and Newton's own life, but for most of us, it's our story too. Both the song and the parable remind us of the open arms, the compassionate heart, and the welcome spirit that describe the nature of the true God who runs to bring us home when we've lost our way.

He's a God I can believe in. He's a God whose mission I can follow.

Continuities. Seeking our mission keeps driving us back to the heart of God. What we find there gives us direction and hope. It makes us listen and make room.

WHAT DO YOU THINK?

1. Why is there an increased interest in atheism in our contemporary world?

2. Do some people reject God because they have not fully investigated who he is?

3. What have you heard people say about God? Where does this thinking come from?

4. What do we learn about God from the story of the prodigal son?

5. Compare the ending of the story in Luke 15 with the conclusion of Dickens's story.

6

THE DREAM IS STILL ALIVE

ISAIAH 11:6-9

David called it the rat house. Born in West Virginia in the late 1990s, David had an older brother and two younger sisters. They were born into a dysfunctional, non-churchgoing family. The father and mother did drugs and drank heavily. The house was filthy. The social worker said when she visited, there was no place to sit in the midst of the spoiled food, the dirty laundry, and the piles of dirt. The windows had no curtains, only old blankets filled with holes. David told me I could tell you his story.

As a preschooler, David did most things for himself. One day, he ran some water to take a bath. As he reached for the soap on the edge of the tub, there was a rat. David was five years old.

Two years later, after school, the social worker waited in front of the elementary school building. He got into her car and saw all his belongings in the back seat. He was entering foster care. David recalls all of it. Mostly, he remembers the rat house.

We wonder about David's future. What will become of him? How do children like David fare in life? How do we help children like David? Where does he fit into God's mission? How do we listen and make room?

When we think of the future, the Old Testament prophets come to mind. Although prophets, they mostly spoke about their present. Occasionally, they would dream about the future. In short, they described what was going on then and what was about to happen or what could happen.

Isaiah wrote in the eighth century BC in a time of great social oppression in Jerusalem. The rich got richer and the poor became poorer. The people in power expressed no outrage about the way the vulnerable were treated. They did not listen to the poor. They never made room for the vulnerable. Isaiah critiqued that culture. In doing so, he had a special concern for children like David who lived in the rat houses of the time, and other vulnerable portions of the population, including widows. In fact, Isaiah often used children in his illustrations.

Writing about hope, he told of a young woman who would bear a son who would be called Immanuel (Isa. 7:14), a child who would bear the government on his shoulders, whose name would be "Wonderful Counselor, Mighty God, Everlasting Father, Prince of Peace" (Isa. 9:6). After his coming, "The wolf shall dwell with the lamb, and the leopard shall lie down with the kid . . . and a little child shall lead them." Also, "The cow and the bear shall feed; their young shall lie down together; and the lion shall eat straw like the ox. The sucking child shall play over the hole of the asp, and the weaned child shall put his hand on the adder's den" (Isa. 11:6–8).

God's language about the future always amazes us. The dead will be raised. There will be new heavens and a new earth. There will be no more tears and no more death. He impresses us in the same way with this passage about animals and children.

- Natural predators coexist peacefully: the wolf and the lamb, the leopard and the goat, the calf and the lion, the cow and the bear, and the lion and the ox.
- A young child lives in the midst of the dangerous animals. The child takes charge of the wolf and the leopard, who under normal conditions might well eat the child. The baby plays with snakes and even puts a hand inside the hole of a poisonous snake.

The scene recalls two works of art. Edward Hicks was a Quaker minister in eastern Pennsylvania in the early nineteenth century. He had no marketable skills, and since Quaker ministers did not receive payment for their preaching, Hicks became a painter to support his family. Over one hundred times, Hicks painted this scene from Isaiah. He called it *The Peaceable Kingdom*. One hangs in the National Gallery in Washington,

DC. He loved children and gave a visual expression of the children with wild animals.

The other work of art reflecting this scene is the 2006 action thriller *Snakes on a Plane,* directed by David Ellis and starring Samuel Jackson. The government is transporting a witness to a gangster killing to Los Angeles on a commercial jet. The gangster secretly arranges for a large crate of venomous snakes to be placed in cargo. Midflight, the crate opens. Snakes appear in the bathrooms, drop out of the luggage racks, and appear in the cockpit. It seems more of a horror picture than an action thriller.

But the movie and Isaiah capitalize on the same fear. Snakes bite people. Lions eat oxen. Lambs are not safe around wolves. What is Isaiah saying with these remarkable images?

Isaiah addresses the issue of injustice in eighth-century Jerusalem. He predicts a leader will arise who will confront the inequities. He writes, "But with righteousness he shall judge the poor, and decide with equity for the meek of the earth; and he shall smite the earth with the rod of his mouth, and with the breath of his lips he shall slay the wicked" (Isa. 11:4). Witnessing the abuse of the poor, injustices toward widows, and the oppression of the orphans, Isaiah announces that it will end.

With this remarkable language about animals and children, the prophet told them what might be. He dreamed about how the world could be. In describing the most impossible kind of world, Isaiah made the point that with God, this can happen.

He called people not to give up on the dream of a peaceable kingdom. Children can live in a safe world. Hearts can be healed. Families can be restored. Cities can be safe. The sex trade of teenage girls can end. The abuse of foster children can stop. Hard hearts can be softened. The "not goods" can be repaired. We can listen, and we can make room.

The dream of the child playing with the snakes makes us think outside the box. Instead of saying that I can't listen or I can't find room, we think of the wolf playing with the lamb. Instead of only seeing the "not goods," we see the good of a leopard cuddling up with a kid. Instead of joining Humpty Dumpty in a dirge on the world's brokenness, we see the cow and the bear jointly enjoying a meal. It's a dream that stretches our thinking, makes us listen, and opens our doors.

Isaiah tells us that God can make the most unlikely things a reality. Wolves can live with lambs. Babies can play with snakes. The impossible dream must be kept alive. Do not give up on the dream of the peaceable kingdom.

~~⌒

The Hughes family lived in public housing in Atlanta. In the summer of 2011, the mother put her little eighteen-month-old boy in a pot of boiling water. He sustained second- and third-degree burns on his feet, legs, and genitals.

Maybe there are some things that God can't do. Maybe the whole business of a child playing over the hole of an asp is just a metaphor that needs some good reality. We start to rebuild the walls of the box we had dared to think outside of.

In midsummer, the doctors started skin grafts. Georgia Agape Child Care Agency took custody of the Hughes' children and removed their terror. The kids moved into a red brick house with beige siding and attended the Campus Church of Christ. The little boy dropped into boiling water in June ran around like a happy toddler in September.

The dream is still alive.

Marta grew up in a depressed area of Mexico. At fifteen, a man promised her a good job in a restaurant in the United States. She agreed and flew to Boston. When she arrived, he told her she had to pay for the flight. She could not. He sold her to a man who listed her as a sex slave on Craigslist. They drugged her and told her if she didn't cooperate, they would harm her family in Mexico.

Maybe God can't fix all problems.

A friend of mine intervened and rescued Marta from the sex trafficking business. Shortly afterward, Marta was working on her GED and was a faithful member of a New York City church. I listened to Marta tell her story.

The dream is still alive.

Remember my West Virginia friend David who lived in the rat house? What happened to him? God is not yet finished with that story. My good friends Chris and Patty opened their home to David and his sisters.

David became a Christian. I was there the Sunday his sister was baptized into Christ.

No more rats.

The dream is still alive.

> **Continuities.** Isaiah's outlandish language makes a critical point about God's mission to fix the broken world. It reminds us that most people will consider it impossible. If it's impossible, why even listen, let alone make room? Despite our reluctance, God in our own time accomplishes what we thought could not be done. Isaiah's dream for the future allows us to think about listening and making room in new ways. Not all are called to be like Chris and Patty, who adopted those three children, or like my friend in New York who worked in the dangerous world of sex trafficking. Not everybody needs to be a foster parent. Some of us may be like Isaiah, who kept the dream alive; while others may have the skills of the doctors and social workers in Atlanta who helped the Hughes baby. It's a call to find our own way to listen and make room.

WHAT DO YOU THINK?

1. What reaction do you have to Isaiah's scene of the peaceable kingdom?

2. Share a story of an impossible situation with a positive outcome. Share a story of an impossible situation with a negative outcome.

3. What reaction do you have to the rat house, the boiling water story, and sex trafficking?

4. In the three stories above, God uses men and women to rescue boys and girls. How is God using someone you know to listen, make space, and rescue a life?

7

WIND CHANGERS

JAMES 1:26-27

Monitoring public opinion, keeping track of popular culture, and collecting data on what people buy or the websites they visit capture the attention of many people. Some collect the information in order to make a profit. Others seek to know which way the wind blows so they can get in front of it and cruise to success. It's not uncommon for people to lead lives based on what they think are the current trends.

What do the marketers say about listening to children? Does it make good business sense to make room? What is the return on investment for mending the world's broken people? Those are good questions. I think it boils down to one issue.

The Bible tells of people who did not go with the current trends, who did not check to see which way the wind was blowing. It tells of those who became wind changers. They knew their course and never wavered.

Joshua didn't take a poll about who wanted to make a covenant. Instead, he changed the wind. He issued this statement:

> Now therefore fear the LORD, and serve him in sincerity and in faithfulness; put away the gods which your fathers served beyond the River, and in Egypt, and serve the LORD. And if you be unwilling to serve the LORD, choose this day whom you will serve, whether the gods your fathers served in the region beyond the River, or the gods of the Amorites in whose land you dwell; but as for me and my house, we will serve the LORD. (Josh. 24:14–15)

Joshua said, "Here's where I'm going." He did not check which way the culture was drifting. Instead, he asked, "Who is coming along?"

The prophet Micah did not set his direction based on polls or surveys. He was a wind changer when he said, "He has showed you, O man, what is good; and what does the LORD require of you but to do justice, and to love kindness, and to walk humbly with your God?" (Mic. 6:8). He set his goal and never wavered. Micah said, "Here's where I'm going. Who is coming along?"

Jesus did not have a consultant that advised him on the current culture or which way the political and social winds were blowing. Instead, he found his direction in an old text that announced how the Spirit of the Lord had anointed him to preach good news to the poor and release to the captives (Luke 4:18–19). He set his compass by the divine North Pole. Jesus said, "Here's where I'm going. Who is coming along?"

Changing the wind has nothing to do with putting up your finger to see which direction the breeze is blowing. It does not use polls, marketing surveys, or consultants. Rather, the pages of Scripture reveal people who went against the grain, who dreamed of the way God wanted things, and who went out and changed the wind.

Back in the 1960s, a preacher named Ira North decided to change the wind. He preached a sermon he simply called "Benevolence." He presented it at lectureships, at area-wide gatherings, and at his home church.[1]

In the 1940s, his congregation began meeting in a tent. They barely had enough money to keep house for God. Then, Ira North did an unusual thing. He didn't put up his finger to check the wind direction. He didn't take a poll. Instead, he read the Bible and then met with church leaders. He asked them, "What are we doing for the poor? We're out preaching to everybody in town, but we are not out practicing like the local service club."

He went on to critique the church culture:

When you mention the Church of Christ, people say, "You are the ones who think everybody's going to hell except you." I've held meetings in places where you couldn't drag a man into a church building. Let's change the image, so that when you

---

[1] Ira North, "Benevolence," Eden Records (Nashville: Christian Publishing Company, 1966).

mention the Church of Christ, people say, "I know them. They practice what they preach. They take care of the poor, the lowly, the downtrodden. They look after the homeless, the abandoned children in town. I may not agree with all their doctrines, but one thing for sure, I thank God for the Church of Christ."

Ira changed the wind. The Madison Church of Christ, where he preached, opened a children's home on the church property. They were soon spending one thousand dollars a week (a lot in the 1960s) on the poor. Their benevolence program had seven deacons to administer it.

He told the congregation, "When a church decides to bring its practice up to its preaching, the hand of God will move in that congregation." Soon, the Madison Church of Christ was the largest Church of Christ in the world.

But that's not all.

Ira North gave the speech across the nation. In the wake of his challenge, new children's homes sprang up. Churches of Christ experienced a growth spurt. The old image fell away, and people began to visit our churches. Ira North was a wind changer. But it didn't originate with him. He dipped deep into Scripture to find the challenge he issued.

He knew about Deuteronomy 10. Israel had camped next to the Promised Land. The invasion was to begin in a few days. Moses gathered the people. He didn't check the wind or poll the people or see what was happening in Palestine. He gave them a dream. He set a vision. He changed the wind.

He described the kind of nation they should be, the kind of communities they should establish, the kind of concerns they should have. He challenged them in this way because of the God they served. Here's one of the greatest descriptions of God in the Bible: "For the LORD your God is God of gods and Lord of lords, the great, the mighty, and the terrible God, who is not partial and takes no bribe" (Deut. 10:17).

Those lines inspired the psalm writers and song composers. The faithful speak of their God in these terms. He is God of gods! He is Lord of lords! But Moses didn't stop there. His description of the core of our divine Father goes on. He told us what is important to the God of gods: "He executes justice for the fatherless and the widow, and loves the sojourner, giving him food and clothing. Love the sojourner therefore; for you were sojourners in the land of Egypt" (Deut. 10:18–19). The Lord of lords has deep concern for the orphan, the widow, and the alien. These lines inspire Joshua to challenge the people, "As for me and my house." They stand behind Micah's ringing words to Jerusalem, "Do justice, love kindness." Jesus draws on these same thoughts when he announces, "He has anointed me to preach good news to the poor." We'll return to those lines later in this book.

One Sunday, Ira North told about a little Native American child found in the Tennessee woods. She lived like an animal. Adults had mistreated her. The state of Tennessee took her to a psychiatric hospital. The director of the institution realized he had a difficult case. He called Ira North and told him, "We have had this child two years. She won't talk. She can't communicate. I think if she had a caring stepmother and a loving adoptive father, I believe it would change her life."

Ira North went back to his church. One Sunday morning in the sermon, he begged somebody to take this little Indian girl. A couple volunteered. After thirty days in their home, she began to smile, and then to talk. Then she changed. She went to Christian camp.

Ira North said, "She always comes by my door. I kiss her on the head. I think she's the prettiest child around."

What was Ira North doing? He was changing the wind. He listened to God. He stood in a line behind Joshua, Micah, Jesus, and a host of others. He knew the Lord of lords cared about the weakest child.

America has huge problems. Many of them concern children. Everywhere we turn, we find neglected, vulnerable, hungry, abandoned children. Many of them grow up to face a life on drugs or incarceration or dependency. We have two choices: We can put up our fingers to see what the polls have to say. Or we can change the wind.

Continuities. In our list of the world's problems and solutions, listening to and making room for vulnerable children might not make the top ten. However, in the end, there is only one poll I'm interested in reading and following: What is God's mission?

WHAT DO YOU THINK?

1. Is the author saying nobody should take polls or listen to public opinion?

2. Make a list of some songs that use lines from the Deuteronomy 10 passage.

3. Is listening and making room for vulnerable children so against the grain of our culture? Explain your answer.

4. Is changing the wind only a role for church leaders?

8

A TIME FOR RENEWAL

ESTHER

Most of us have been to a banquet. People enjoy the food and conversation, have a bit of fun, and then the program begins. Sometimes the group recognizes significant achievements. When it comes to banquets, it's hard not to think of Esther.

The Old Testament book of Esther tells the story of Jews living in Persia during a time of exile from Jerusalem, and it has ten chapters. Those chapters tell about ten banquets.

The first four banquets come right at the beginning. The book opens with the king, Ahasuerus, hosting a national celebration banquet that went on for one hundred and eighty days. Later, the king convened a smaller banquet dinner that lasted a couple of days. Meanwhile, the queen, Vashti, banqueted with a group of women. We'll get to the fourth banquet in a bit.

During the second banquet, Ahasuerus decided to show off his queen, Vashti. She refused to be paraded in front of his guests. The king's advisors urged the king to act, because he couldn't let the queen set such a rebellious precedent. Ahasuerus removed Vashti from the throne.

Besides the Persians, there are two key Jewish people in the story: Mordecai and his adopted daughter, Esther. His decision to adopt his niece had lasting implications for the Jewish people. He watched as she grew into a beautiful young woman. Esther, in time, was selected by Ahasuerus as queen, and she was announced at the fourth banquet.

Sometime after the fourth banquet, Mordecai overheard a plot to assassinate the king. He notified Queen Esther, who passed on the word. When the police investigated, the conspirators were found and hanged.

A short while later, Mordecai encountered the king's top assistant, Haman, who noticed that Mordecai refused to show him the proper respect. In revenge, at a fifth banquet, Haman persuaded the king to issue an edict to kill all the Jews in Persia. They cast lots and picked a date. Mordecai heard of the plan to kill all the Jews, including Esther and him.

Mordecai told Esther about the plan and urged her to go to the king. She pointed out that even the queen cannot approach the king without an invitation, and to do so risked death. Still, Mordecai urged her to action:

> Think not that in the king's palace you will escape any more than all the other Jews. For if you keep silence at such a time as this, relief and deliverance will rise for the Jews from another quarter, but you and your father's house will perish. And who knows whether you have not come to the kingdom for such a time as this? (Esther 4:13–14)

He persuaded Esther, and she called for a fast: "Then I will go to the king, though it is against the law; and if I perish, I perish" (Esther 4:16).

Esther approached the king. He welcomed her and offered her half his kingdom. She requested a banquet with the king and Haman. At that sixth banquet in the book, Esther invited the king and Haman to another banquet.

Prior to that second banquet Esther hosted for the king, the seventh in the book of Esther, two things happened. Haman, overjoyed with the attention of the king and his new queen, encountered the disrespectful Mordecai. In anger, he reported the insult to his wife, who urged Haman to have Mordecai hanged. Haman ordered the seventy-five-foot-high gallows built.

At about the same time, the king, suffering from insomnia, had an aide read the record of memorial deeds and heard the story of Mordecai saving him from the assassins. Learning that Mordecai had not been rewarded, he asked Haman how he should honor a man he wanted to recognize. Haman thought the king wanted to honor him and proposed that the honoree parade around the city on the king's horse. Ahasuerus agreed and told Haman to do exactly that . . . for Mordecai!

At Esther's second banquet with the king and Haman, the king, in a good mood, asked Esther what she wanted. Esther replied that she wanted to live. Astounded, the king asked who sought her life. Esther pointed to a horrified Haman. The king angrily left the room. Haman fell on Esther's couch to plead his case, and when the king reentered, he accused Haman of molesting the queen. The king hanged Haman on the gallows Haman had built for Mordecai.

After Esther's banquets, a couple of important events take place. At the eighth banquet in the book, Mordecai took Haman's place as the king's top aide. Esther and Mordecai persuaded the king to grant the Jews the right to defend themselves in the coming purge. The day arrived, and the purge failed. Over seventy-five thousand Persians died, but no Jews.

The book concludes with two final banquets (nine and ten respectively). The Jews celebrated in a banquet when the king issued the edict allowing them to defend themselves. Then, they convened a second banquet after the defeat of the Persians. With this tenth and final banquet, the Jews established Purim to celebrate their victory.

What do we make of this story that rides on the back of ten banquets?

First, people often observe what's not in this story. None of the names for God appear in the book. Fasting is mentioned, but not prayer. In fact, the book mentions nothing spiritual, nothing about the return to Jerusalem to rebuild the temple, nothing about Scripture, covenant, grace, or justice. Esther is not quoted or mentioned in the New Testament, nor are any manuscripts of the book found among the Dead Sea Scrolls. At first glance, it appears to be a secular book that ends up in the Bible.

Second, the book raises moral concerns. The virgin, unmarried Jewish girl Esther sleeps with Ahasuerus. Esther goes into the king as an unmarried virgin and comes out as a concubine with the title of queen. She does not do what we expect a good Hebrew girl to do.

The book centers on envy, hatred, anger, vindictiveness, and pride, all in a context of religious indifference. Even the "self-defense" of the Jews at the end seems more like vengeance with the 75,800-to-0 casualty report.

The good Jews slaughter men, women, and children without a command from God.

Third, the book is filled with coincidences. Vashti happens to refuse the king's request. Esther happens to be selected queen. Mordecai happens to overhear the assassination plan. Esther happens to put her life on the line. Ahasuerus happens to have insomnia. The king happens to welcome Esther into the court. The king happens to hear the report of Mordecai's deed. Haman happens to build a gallows. The king happens to reenter the banquet when Haman throws himself at Esther. How do we explain the coincidences? What do we do with a book in the Bible about an orphan girl who saves her people without mentioning God? Consider these three observations:

- In a world where God is not mentioned, much like ours, where all events are assigned to some other force, God is still at work. Esther unfolds a theology of the silent providence of God. God does not appear and is not even mentioned by any of the actors, but he directs the whole story.
- In a world where even good people do bad things, God still works. God works in our messy world and works through the most unusual people. He used an orphan who violated the moral law as a means of saving the nation. We should not pretend to be perfect as we walk in front of our friends and neighbors, because just as we see Esther's faults, they see our faults. But neither her faults nor ours keep God from doing his work.
- In a world that seems to ignore orphans and adoptive parents, God still works. Esther lost her parents but was raised by her uncle. Every day, mothers give up their children for adoption. Every day, children go into foster care. Every day, adoptive parents take home a child they did not bear. Every day, a child enters a home not their own.

In some ways, the book of Esther is a book for our time. In a secular world where moral standards have eroded, the number of ignored and vulnerable children and poor continues unabated. Who will listen to their cries? Who will make room for them? Is there any way to fix this brokenness?

Esther reminds us that God is at work in societies just like ours.

We never know where God will work next. It may be in one of these vulnerable children or charitable adults that God does his greatest work in our time.

Who knows? You may have come to the kingdom for such a time as this.

Continuities. This complex story mirrors our own day. It may be one of the Bible's most relevant books in terms of how we stay on mission in a secular culture. Strikingly, the story uses an orphan to call us to our mission.

WHAT DO YOU THINK?

1. Why is a book like Esther in the Bible?

2. Why is God not mentioned in the book?

3. Discuss the author's proposed parallels between Esther and the contemporary world.

4. Describe a situation where God has made you a contemporary of Esther.

5. Have you seen God working behind the scenes in your life, family, church, or community? Explain.

PART 2

LISTENING TO CHILDREN

Listening and making room is much easier to say than to do, much easier to start than to finish, much easier to see in others than to see in oneself. Connecting listening and making room to God's mission of fixing our broken world helps us see how it fits into our worldview. By following the example of Jesus, collaborating with others, and realizing that through our listening and making room God changes lives, we are given a foundation on which to live in this way.

At first glance, listening as a means of accomplishing God's mission for the world may seem incredibly easy. But often, it is difficult. Difficult because we don't live near the people whose voices we need to hear. Difficult because our lives are filled with voices to which we give priority. Difficult because some of those whose voices we need to hear cannot even speak.

In this section on listening, we explore another world we know exists, but which many seldom enter. Once we understand where these voices come from, we more easily find a way to listen to those in similar situations close to us. The Bible contains examples of some of these voices. Even in our Bible study, we find it easier to read past these voices and go on to the material that has more appeal. But the voices are still there, and as the Bible loves to do, these biblical passages give them a voice.

The Bible tells us who inflicts pain on the vulnerable and voiceless. These passages also reflect on what it's like to be a forgotten person or a neglected child.

In learning to hear what these children are saying, the Bible also points to critical ways in which we make room for them. We will take up those issues in the third part of the book, "Listening to God about Children." We will learn to make room by adding blessing, value, a sense of home, and the promise that God will not forget. Making room includes teaching, evangelism, and careful instruction about passing on the faith. All of this comes from the one who listens best: our Father in heaven who cares for all the orphans.

When we listen, we hear pain. If we want to understand pain, there's no better place to start than the book of Hosea. In the next two chapters, this eighth-century BC prophet tutors us on pain.

9

CALM IN THE MIDST OF THE STORM

HOSEA 1-3

Places along the coast are known for their storms. Hurricanes, tsunamis, and tropical storms descend and destroy. They create confusion and chaos. In a sense, the Old Testament book of Hosea tells of storms. Hosea 4:19, 8:7, 12:1, and 13:15 all use storms to make a point. He uses storms as a metaphor for a nation that is out of control. The people of Israel were like victims in the midst of a hurricane. Their sin caused a storm. God's coming destruction would be like a disastrous storm.

But Hosea is also a book about children. The children he describes are caught up in the storms destroying their nation, just as our vulnerable children get caught in the bitter winds of our culture. In Hosea 9:10–17, Hosea prays the only prayer in the book. He starts, "Give them, O LORD," and then can't continue. He can't say the "Amen." I think that Hosea must have cried because it hurt so much to finish his prayer. Then he prays this line: "Give them a miscarrying womb and dry breasts" (Hosea 9:14). Hosea knows that God's punishment will be so severe that he will not allow them to have children to witness such events. In the coming punishment for the sins of Ephraim, there will be no more conceptions, no pregnancies, no births. If children are born, they will die as infants. If a boy makes it to adolescence, parents will slaughter their own son. Adult decisions have significant negative consequences for children, and he uses the pain of children to describe the result of adult decisions.

But in the midst of this stormy language and in the midst of the children's situation, Hosea describes a great calm. He tells the troubled Israelites how to find calm, how to locate shelter from the winds. It comes in his opening chapters.

God instructed Hosea to marry an adulterous woman named Gomer (Hosea 1:2). He did, and she bore him a little boy. Later, she was expecting again, and this time Gomer had a girl. The third child was another little boy. Hosea found out that the last two were not his. Then they argued in front of the children. Hosea locked the door and put up a fence between his house and the lover's house, but it didn't stop Gomer. She left and moved in with the other man. We don't know how long she was gone. Hosea became a single parent raising the three children. He changed the diapers of the child his wife had by his neighbor. He taught a child to walk while her mother was in somebody else's bed.

Hosea went through all this chaos because God asked him to do it. God made the request so that Israel would feel the pain that God feels when they reject him. Hosea's book describes the broken heart of God by telling of the pain of children.

Hosea did a strange thing to express the pain. He gave the children terrible names. He called the oldest boy Jezreel. It was the name of a notorious battlefield. It would be like naming a child Auschwitz or Gettysburg or 9/11. It communicated "You're going to get it." The little girl was called "Not Loved." It might be like naming your daughter Ugly or Dogface. The name said, "I don't care what happens to you." He named the third child "Not My People," which would be similar to naming a baby Rejected or Beat It or Go Away. It said, "You're not my kid."

Imagine when Hosea took the family to market. There's Auschwitz, Ugly, and Go Away. Every time he called them to supper, every night he put them to bed, every time he sent them off to school, every time he heard the neighborhood children tease them, it ripped out his heart.

Do you want to know what our sins do to God? Call your little girl Ugly for a week. Nickname your son Stupid. Stand by while the kids call your child Dog. That's how God feels when we sin.

It amazes us that Hosea would do such a thing. How could a father use such terrible names? How could God expect such behavior? Why did this family unfold in this way? It's all to help us understand the length God goes to let us know what it's like to be God when his people are unfaithful.

God knows about human pain. He knows how the vulnerable suffer. He sees the hurt adults cause children. He hears what those who serve abandoned children hear. He is frustrated by what frustrates those who work with unwanted children around the world. Then in the midst of the storms of pain, he tells the story of calm.

I don't know anybody in the Bible that describes life's storms better than Hosea. He knows the strong winds of discouragement, the pain of life's hurricanes, and the bruising of the battering storms. He knows how storms break young lives, how the wind blows away their hopes, and how the twisters tear children away from those they love.

But in the middle of the storm comes calm. God tells Hosea, "Go find Gomer and bring her home." *You mean the woman who caused this pain? You mean the woman who sleeps around? You mean the one who deserted the kids and me?*

God says, "Yes. Go love her again." Hosea went and found Gomer in whatever bed she had landed. He paid the price, brought her home, and made her his wife . . . again.

The calm comes from God. When we have done everything wrong, when we've turned our back on God, when we have flirted with other gods, God takes us back. When we hurt children, when we ignore their cries, and when we turn aside from the vulnerable, God takes us back. Listen to his marriage offer in Hosea 2:19–20. It was first written to Hosea, but God copied the message to all of us who have betrayed him:

> And I will betroth you to me forever;
> I will betroth you to me in righteousness and in justice,
> in steadfast love, and in mercy.
> I will betroth you to me in faithfulness;
> and you shall know the Lord.

Life has its storms. Those who listen to at-risk children and who hear the voices of the vulnerable face the winds and rains as much as anybody.

Hosea reminds us we are not alone. In the middle of every storm is a God calling us into the shelter of his love and faithfulness.

Hosea amazes us. He uses the pain of children to tell us two things: Adult decisions hurt children. The pain these children experience gives us insight into the hurt God endures when we turn away from his love.

Hosea marched three little children onto the stage of history, and each one bore a name that preached a sermon every time they were called to supper. They were names that made their lives painful beyond imagination. The message they carried is still relevant.

> For I desire steadfast love and not sacrifice,
> the knowledge of God, rather than burnt offerings. (Hosea 6:6)

Continuities. Hosea uses the language of pain. It's an important language to learn if we are going to hear the cries of children. In the next chapter, Hosea reveals the identity of the one who speaks the language of pain.

WHAT DO YOU THINK?

1. Share examples of unusual names that parents give their children.

2. How do you respond to the names Hosea gives to the three children in the story?

3. How do adults cause children pain?

4. What do you think of Hosea's prayer in 9:10–17?

5. How does Hosea 2:19–20 give you peace?

6. What can we learn about God from Hosea's experiences?

10

STORM IN THE
MIDST OF CALM

HOSEA 11:8-11

Most people know the bitter feelings of a broken heart. A couple breaks up, and they feel the loneliness, pain, and regret. After the funeral, the surviving spouse returns home to the empty house, the empty car, the empty bed, and to emptiness in general. An adult child leaves the hospital where his parent just died, and he experiences a new kind of aloneness. A young child leaves home to go into foster care, her world and her heart broken. A teenage girl gets caught in sex trafficking, and she loses all contact with family and the joys of life. In each case, the person feels vulnerable, broken, and alone.

In our "not good" world, we hear the voices of the brokenhearted. We hear of their pain and rejection. We learn of the vulnerability and loneliness. It makes us ponder how we should handle this brokenness.

It also makes us wonder if God hears this brokenness. How did God feel when Adam and Eve ate the fruit he told them not to eat? What happened in his heart when he saw the golden calf? What effect did it have when David sent a message to Bathsheba and ended up in bed with her? Where was God when Judas said, "That's him."

What goes through the divine heart when a newly baptized young man clicks on a porn site the next week, or when a deacon signs a contract based on a lie, or when the Sunday school teacher leads a study of 1 Corinthians 13 and then treats everybody she meets with meanness?

Perhaps no Scripture gives more insight into God's heart than the prophet Hosea. These fourteen chapters come from the eighth century BC. We often find it difficult to read because he utilizes so many agricultural and nature images that are not part of our experience. He writes in troubled historical times with details difficult to keep straight.

But there's something important here. It reads more like a love letter than systematic theology; more like a peek into God's diary than a read of his sermon. It's more a journey through his heart than a trip through his mind. We see the story of a broken heart more than pages of dusty history.

Compare the Gospels with Hosea. The Gospels tell us what God would be like if he were a man, how he would walk, talk, live, and laugh if he were among us. The Gospels put skin and clothes on God.

Hosea moves in a different direction. It tells us in human terms what it's like to be God. It uses our emotions, concerns, and pains to describe the experience of God. The Gospels transport God to earth; Hosea transports us to heaven. The Gospels open a door for God to walk among us. Hosea is a window through which we see God.

Hosea can't be reduced to a set of propositions or three quick points. Hosea spins a great allegory. In chapters 1–3, God tells Hosea to marry an unfaithful woman named Gomer. In chapter 11, a similar event occurs when, after Gomer deserts the family, Hosea raises the kids by himself. Hosea teaches them to walk and takes them to school, but the kids turn out bad.

God is like a father to Israel. God called Israel home from Egypt, taught him to walk, kissed his hurts when he fell. But Israel was a rebellious child. In Hosea 11:3, God laments: "I took them up in my arms; but they did not know that I healed them." Later in verse 7, God agonizes: "My people are bent on turning away from me."

It's every parent's nightmare. The call comes from the police station. They discover the porn sites in the cache. The child's face turns bitter and the language ugly: "I hate you. Get out of my life."

Your heart is broken. "But I bore you, I raised you, I taught you to walk. I healed you. I poured my life into you." All the dreams crushed and the hopes smashed.

If you can imagine that horrible experience, then you know what God feels like, what happens in his heart every time you intentionally sin, and how your life touches his.

Two things shock us about Hosea's allegory. First, we're shocked at the extent to which God pushes his prophet Hosea. God tells Hosea to marry a harlot. Gomer didn't wear white at their wedding. Some people came to the wedding to see what she looked like during the day. When Hosea walked down the aisle, he passed men who had spent time with his wife. The man at the market could have been the father of two or three of his children.

Gomer was sexually experienced. She'd been sleeping around. Even after they married, she was sleeping around. God told Hosea to take her back after she refused to quit. No congregation would hire a minister who did what God told Hosea to do. That's why we disfellowship people. That's why we fire preachers. Rightly so, because it's wrong.

But God tells Hosea to marry such a woman because what's at stake is understanding sin. Hosea could not reach the people. The more Hosea said, the more they sinned. They didn't even know that what they were doing was wrong. So, God told Hosea to marry a harlot. Give your children offensive names. Drag your wife out of another man's bed. Let your teens become rebellious.

Why? God tells Hosea to do these things so Israel can see exactly what their actions do to God. It's the story of God's broken heart.

The second shock wave coming out of these chapters conveys the degree to which God experiences emotional upheaval. We read about other times that grieve God's heart and events that make him angry, but none of it quite measures up to what we learn about God in Hosea 11:

> My people are bent on turning away from me; so they are
> appointed to the yoke, and none shall remove it. How can I give
> you up, O Ephraim! How can I hand you over, O Israel! How
> can I make you like Admah! How can I treat you like Zeboiim!
> My heart recoils within me, my compassion grows warm and
> tender. I will not execute my fierce anger, I will not again destroy
> Ephraim; for I am God and not man, the Holy One in your
> midst, and I will not come to destroy. (Hosea 11:7–9)

God can see his people turning away. At first, he decides to let them bear the yoke of punishment. "I will not respond even if they call." Then, he questions his own decision. He speaks as a parent who faces the rejection of his own child, but he can't give up. His heart boils over, filled with a storm. "You are my son. I can't give you up." Then, he drops the parental language. "I am not a wounded husband or a forgotten father. I am the holy one. I will not destroy. I will take them back."

Hosea says if you think God remains untouched by what we do, then think again. Hosea opens a window into God's heart. What we see is a heart broken by human unfaithfulness. It's broken by you and by me. But the storm in God's heart turns to calm. Out of the wind comes grace. Out of the struggle comes mercy. Out of the devastation comes salvation.

The wonder of all the prophetic books is hope. God is like a father punishing a rebellious son, who can order the destruction of Samaria and Jerusalem, but each prophet ends on a word of hope. Hosea ends with images of agricultural plenty.

Hosea reminds us that after every storm comes calm. After every bad comes good. Even when God is caught up in the storm, even when darkness covers Calvary, even when we're not sure there will be a tomorrow, God comes with grace, mercy, and peace.

Understanding pain within this promise prepares us to listen to the pain of children. The next six chapters explore the nature of those cries.

Continuities. God knows about pain. We hear the cries of his pain. The more we learn about the heart of God, the easier it is to listen and to understand the cries of pain around us. Too often, that pain is caused by the adults of our world, a subject which the next chapter explores.

WHAT DO YOU THINK?

1. God asked Hosea to marry a harlot and then raise her children. What do you think of that request? Can you think of other outlandish requests that God has made?

2. What do you think of the comparison between the Gospels and Hosea?

3. How does Hosea change your perspective on your own sins?

4. How does God feel about how the contemporary world treats vulnerable children?

5. God's heart is broken by human unfaithfulness. What situations are you aware of that break God's heart today?

11

DANGER AHEAD— UNSAFE FOR CHILDREN

ISAIAH 10:1–4

Gus's Bar and Grill sat on a corner of Princess Street in York, Pennsylvania. During a recent three-year period, the police were called for some emergency event at the bar six hundred seventy-seven times. The establishment claimed to be a grill, but the only food they served was microwaved soup. Locals knew it was a headquarters for drugs, violence, prostitution, and evil.

Larry grew up in the nearby neighborhood. His father frequented the bar, and one night he was shot and killed in the street across from Gus's. Larry accepted his father's death as part of urban life in York, the one-time capital of the United States.

A woman I'll call Allison works as an internist in a large city in the southwestern part of the United States. Nearly every day, she sees inner-city girls in her office. Most are pregnant. About half of them tell Allison that the father of their child is the girl's own father. Allison goes home and cries every night.

The stories go on. They include teenage girls caught in the sex trade, eight-year-olds beaten by their fathers, hundreds of thousands of children in foster care, women battered by the men in their lives, and millions of children dying from preventable causes.

All of it creates dissonance. Gus's Bar and Grill serves death and destruction while two miles away, people enjoy the luxury of fine dining in a four-star restaurant. Allison treats a thirteen-year-old with her father's baby while across town, another father complains that his son doesn't get to start on the third-grade soccer team. Children in the Bronx die from crime while six subway stops away in Manhattan, children the same age swim in the penthouse pool. Child care agencies turn away foster children every day while a nearby church drops them from their budget in order to build a new gymnasium to serve their middle-class neighborhood.

The questions are clear: How can the poor and rich exist side by side? Why do so many people ignore the cries of the poor? Why does evil seem to triumph over good? Why do so many of us turn a deaf ear to the cries of the hurting. Why do so many ignore the places like Gus's Bar and Grill?

The first dozen chapters of Isaiah describe the same kind of world. The wealthy and the poor lived side by side. The haves ignored the have-nots. Those in power oppressed those without power.

The eighth century BC in Jerusalem was a violent time. The streets were violent. A series of wars left many homes without fathers and husbands. Farm families found themselves without a male figure. Mother and children had to go it alone in a patriarchal world.

People in power saw it as an opportunity to make money. They loaned funds to widows, and when they couldn't pay it back, they took the widows' farms. While the wealthy enjoyed the land that belonged to the widow or the orphan, the mother and child languished.

Isaiah responded to the inequity, to the rich ignoring the poor and the wealthy enjoying life down the street from the starving orphan. Here is what he says in Isaiah 10:1–4:

> Woe to those who decree iniquitous decrees, and the writers
> who keep writing oppression, to turn aside the needy from jus-
> tice and to rob the poor of my people of their right, that widows
> may be their spoil, and that they may make the fatherless their
> prey! What will you do on the day of punishment, in the storm
> which will come from afar? To whom will you flee for help,
> and where will you leave your wealth? Nothing remains but to
> crouch among the prisoners or fall among the slain. For all this
> his anger is not turned away and his hand is stretched out still.

The passage has three parts. *First come five accusations.* Woe to the people who make this legal. You deny fair treatment to those most in need. You take what belongs to the poor and make yourself richer. The money in your bank account should belong to the widow. You hunt orphans like animals to be killed.

Then come three questions. How will you defend yourself before God? Where will you hide in the storm God sends? Will your wealth benefit you when you stand before God?

The third part of the passage is the one verdict. He begins, "For all this"— that is, for mistreating the poor, ignoring the plight of vulnerable children, and causing their pain—"God's anger" is not satisfied and will not be satisfied until all is made right. Moreover, "God's hand" that reaches out to save the vulnerable is poised to destroy those guilty of injustice. It's the fifth time in twelve chapters that Isaiah issues the exact same verdict.

This is a dangerous text. It's the preacher accusing the president. It's God taking on the corporate world. It's a booming voice for the powerless. It's a call to do right in the midst of high profits.

So, what is the point? How does it help us? The passage reminds us not to lose our sense of outrage. It's a call not to let the world blind us to suffering. Isaiah calls us to listen to the voices of those in pain. It's a reminder that the "not good" world is just across town and down the street. It challenges us to have the courage to stand up and say certain things are wrong. They have always been wrong, and they will always be wrong, and no matter how much an affluent society says otherwise, they are still wrong.

The text says: Do not close your eyes. Do not turn your head away. Do not numb your senses. Do not ignore what you hear. Do not make the horrible into the honorable. Do not turn starvation into hunger. Do not reduce rejection to loneliness. Do not allow evil to be the inevitable side effect of capitalism. Don't lose sensitivity to what God considers right and just and holy and pure and true.

Isaiah's lines remind us to announce danger. The pharmaceutical industry has small print that tells us of the danger of the medicine we take. Every electrical appliance has a warning label. Signs on the road tell of a potential danger around the curve. Isaiah reminds us of the dangers of oppressing the poor and vulnerable, the widow and the orphan.

As a young minister, I was asked to speak at a major lectureship among Churches of Christ. It was my first time to speak on such an important program. The focus that year fell on the Gospel of Luke. They asked me to do an evening lecture of Luke 3. The man with two coats should share one. Tax collectors should not abuse the system. Soldiers must not rob anyone through violence.

The study for that lecture changed my life. I began to understand what God was talking about from the beginning to the end of the Bible. For the first time, I came face-to-face with the meaning of righteousness and justice. I understood why James ended the New Testament with a definition of pure religion that meant taking care of widows and orphans.

As I spoke, a close friend of mine was sitting on my right about halfway up in the seating area. When the service was over and my lecture was finished, he heard the person behind him say, "Well, that lecture ought to satisfy the bleeding hearts." The urge not to listen is everywhere. Those telling us not to get upset are in every crowd.

Ira North of the Madison, Tennessee, Church of Christ told a story about being in his office one day. His secretary came in and said, "Brother North, come and look at what somebody donated for the poor." Ira went into the hallway and poked through the box left for the benevolence room. "My, my, I wouldn't give those things away in the name of any organization. I'm certainly not going to give rags away in the name of Jesus." The next Sunday in the pulpit, he told the church that they would not give junk and cast-off clothing in the name of Jesus.

What was going on in the Madison pulpit? It was outrage. It was a voice proclaiming what he had heard. It was a call to make room. It was a voice that echoed Isaiah's outrage at injustice.

I've known Craig Wolf since he was in the ninth grade. He now manages the YMCA in York, Pennsylvania. The Y is down the street from Gus's Bar and Grill. He met Larry just after his father died in front of Gus's tavern. Craig knew if the city was going to be a safe place for children, Gus's had to go. He went to see Gus. "How much will it cost me to buy your bar and grill?" Gus wanted a quarter of a million dollars. Gus overpriced his establishment to keep Craig away. But Craig's outrage would not allow him to keep silent.

Craig went to the liquor board and the police. They cooperated and legitimately shut Gus down for short periods of time due to Gus's violations of the law. His business plummeted. Craig went back to see Gus and asked, "How much now?" They agreed on one hundred and ten thousand dollars.

A few months later, when I visited Craig, I stood in front of what was once Gus's tavern. It was being remodeled into a neighborhood grocery store. The YMCA owns it. They also own the house across the street where Larry's father was killed.

It would have made Isaiah smile. God was surely pleased.

But evil continues to exist, and so do these words of Isaiah: "For all this his anger is not turned away and his hand is stretched out still." God is listening. Are you?

> **Continuities.** Just because we do not experience the pain of oppression does not mean it does not exist or is not worth hearing. Our world is no better than Isaiah's. We continue to pass laws and maintain standards that make children cry out in pain. Isaiah calls us not to lose our sense of outrage. It's not the way it's supposed to be in God's very good world.

WHAT DO YOU THINK?

1. Look through a recent news magazine or newspaper for stories of vulnerable people. What is their situation?

2. Why did Isaiah speak out against the wealthy and powerful people in eighth-century Jerusalem?

3. Identify a place like Gus's Bar and Grill where you live. What role does it play in your community?

4. Brainstorm with your Sunday school class, small group, or other members of your congregation about what you might do concerning the place you identified above.

12

EVERYBODY WINS

EPHESIANS 2:11–22; MARK 10:45; LUKE 6:36, 19:10

Timothy Kinney grew up in Cheviot Township outside Cincinnati, Ohio. He remembers during the civil rights movement, his father, James, and others from his church went to the city council to ask them to remove the law that no black person could be outside on the streets after dark. The council refused, saying that no black people lived in their township, so any African American there after dark was up to no good.

Kinney found an African American family willing to move into the township. Afterward, they returned to the city council to have the law abolished. Reluctantly, the council made the change. The whole incident disturbed James Patrick Kinney, and he wrote the poem "The Cold Within":

> Six humans trapped by happenstance
> In bleak and bitter cold.
> Each one possessed a stick of wood
> Or so the story's told.
>
> Their dying fire in need of logs
> The first man held his back
> For of the faces round the fire
> He noticed one was black.
>
> The next man looking 'cross the way
> Saw one not of his church

And couldn't bring himself to give
The fire his stick of birch.

The third one sat in tattered clothes.
He gave his coat a hitch.
Why should his log be put to use
To warm the idle rich?

The rich man just sat back and thought
Of the wealth he had in store
And how to keep what he had earned
From the lazy, shiftless poor.

The black man's face bespoke revenge
As the fire passed from his sight.
For all he saw in his stick of wood
Was a chance to spite the white.

The last man of this forlorn group
Did nought except for gain.
Giving only to those who gave
Was how he played the game.

Their logs held tight in death's still hands
Was proof of human sin.
They didn't die from the cold without
They died from the cold within.

The poem describes our world. We live in divided communities, each filled with its own isolation, violence, and distrust. We line up opposite each other: white and black, rich and poor, urban and rural, educated and uneducated, white collar and blue collar, and liberal and conservative. There is a slash between us/them. We sit around the same fire and never talk. We warm ourselves with the same heat but never listen.

Contrast all that with these lines:

So then you are no longer strangers and sojourners, but you are fellow citizens with the saints and members of the household of God, built upon the foundation of the apostles and prophets, Christ Jesus himself being the cornerstone, in whom the whole structure is joined together and grows into a holy temple in the Lord; in whom you also are built into it for a dwelling place of God in the Spirit. (Eph. 2:19–22)

The six men around the fire were strangers. Ephesians says we're no longer strangers. The six in Kinney's poem lacked hope. Ephesians says we're filled with hope. The six had rejected each other. Ephesians talks about fellow citizens. The six all sat around the same fire, but they were alienated from each other. Ephesians says we're members of the same household. The six were filled with hate. Ephesians reports we are filled with love.

The book of Ephesians describes the church. The people who are "in Christ" make up the body of Christ. God's plan for uniting the isolated and fragmented segments of the human race was the church. The church!

At a seminar in Washington, DC, I met John DiIulio, who worked for the Bush White House before returning to his role as professor at the University of Pennsylvania. In one of John's lectures with us, he talked about the violence and fragmentation of our nation. He decried the moral poverty and the death rate of urban teens. Then he offered a solution, a way to bring people together, a way to stop the violence, a means of ending the isolation. He challenged us to start one thousand new churches.

That's the point of Ephesians. The mystery was hidden for ages. It was a means of bringing people together. It was the church. People as different as Jew and Gentile, as Scythian and Roman, as master and slave, could all come together in the church.

Harold Trulear served as vice president of Public/Private Ventures, one of the nation's leading youth policy research organizations. He spent decades studying the urban areas from New York City to Philadelphia. He served as a seminary professor. He cited research showing that the source of the most volunteer hours in the organizations seeking the betterment of the city was the church. More people from churches give of their time than any other social organization. He calls the church the first responders to the city's ills.[1]

---

[1] James R. Wilburn, ed., *Faith and Public Policy* (Lanham: Lexington Books, 2002), 66.

James Kinney's poem leaves us asking, What can we do about the cold within? God's answer comes in Ephesians: the church. He calls us to be the body of Christ, not the disconnected bodies around the fire. It's a call to make friends. It's a call to heal, not just do first aid. It's a call to peace, not just a cease-fire. It's a call to build a temple, not tents in the wilderness. It's a call for a dwelling place, not just a bus stop on a busy corner.

Whatever our ministry, whatever our goal, whatever our work, it must revolve around the church.

Jesus built his church as an offensive institution to challenge the "gates of hell" (Matt. 16:18 KJV). It's not a sealed-off fortress but an attacking organization. It's a spiritual army confronting the bastions of evil. It's the joined-together ministering to the left-out. Its fellow citizens ripping up fences. It's the family of God breaking down barriers.

For several years, I worked with an inner-city minister named Anthony. A member of his urban congregation came down with AIDS. She had no family and no support. She was not the same race or economic status or cultural background as Anthony and his family, and they had to make a decision. They could play it safe or be the church. When Sherry became too weak to care for herself, she moved into the house with Anthony and his family. There in the middle of their living room with Anthony, his wife, and two children gathered around, Sherry passed away. This circle was much different than the one in Kinney's poem. This circle is about listening, inclusion, healing, acceptance, and love.

This circle is called the church.

Continuities. Our practice of being church falls short of God's plan for the church. If the vulnerable adults and children of the world are not in our congregations or not welcome in our congregations, it raises critical questions: Are we serving as Jesus served? Do we show the same mercy shown to us? Are we seeking the lost? In other words, do we hear the same cries that God hears?

WHAT DO YOU THINK?

1. Describe your response to the poem "The Cold Within." How would other people in your community respond?

2. Think of a term that best describes your congregation. Consider these: country club, outreach center, fort, welcome center, army of God. How would Paul describe a congregation?

3. Why are some people not welcome in some churches?

4. What can we do to make our churches more welcoming?

5. Are churches some of the first responders in your community? In what ways?

13

ENGRAVING A
CHILD'S HEART

JEREMIAH 17:1-4

In his book *Beggars and Thieves,* Mark Fleisher tells about a conversation he had with members of a gang in Los Angeles. The gang called themselves Chitty Chitty Bang Bang after a song about urban violence. In talking to one young gang member named Body Count, Fleisher asked where the boy got such a name. He replied, "When da shootin's ova' das what I do. Coun' da bodies."[1]

Violence and crime among children touch all of us. It's news we don't like to hear. The girl at the prom delivers a baby in the bathroom, cleans herself up, deserts the baby, and goes back to the dance. Another girl gives birth to a baby in her bedroom, puts the live infant in a plastic garbage sack, and throws it in the dumpster behind the family house. Young men participating in gang initiation go looking to murder any innocent driver who blinks his headlights. The potential gang member pulls his gun and kills the driver. A teenager seeking money for drugs robs a convenience store, leaving the clerk dead. We have grown frustrated with the heavily armed teenager walking into a school with guns blazing.

Why all the violence? Where does it lead? Where does it come from? What can we do?

---

[1] Mark S. Fleisher, *Beggars and Thieves: Lives of Urban Street Criminals* (Madison: University of Wisconsin Press, 1995), 143.

I spent some time with A. C. Wharton, former public defender and mayor of Memphis, Tennessee. He told me that on his way to church many Sundays, he stops at the local city jail. He visits some of the young men, offering words of encouragement. As he left one Sunday, he heard the church bells ringing. He realized that the young men he left behind would likely never go to church again.

The prophet Jeremiah writes about such violent times. He lived in Jerusalem during a time of increasing unrest and violence. When the Babylonians laid siege, conditions inside the walls disintegrated to the point that people treated others in unspeakable ways. Jeremiah 15–17 focuses directly and indirectly on how the violence affected children. He speaks of how their "sons and daughters" would die violent deaths or because of their behavior succumb to terrible maladies (Jer. 16:3–4, 18:21).

We gasp at the language. He announces the funerals of children. He tells of deadly diseases taking young lives. He speaks of a time when no one comes to bury the dead children, whose corpses are left to the vultures.

We shake our heads trying to figure out why such language appears in the Bible and why it associates such horrors with God. Jeremiah anticipated our despair and offers this explanation:

> The sin of Judah is written with a pen of iron; with a point of
> diamond it is engraved on the tablet of their heart, and on the
> horns of their altars, while their children remember their altars
> and their Asherim, beside every green tree, and on the high hills.
> (Jer. 17:1–2)

What sad language. He drew a terrible image. Parents took a primitive writing instrument and with this tool, they engraved their sins onto their children's hearts. Their written words showed no love or sentimentality. They did not write, "I love you" or "May you have a great life" or "You are more precious to me than anything." Instead, they wrote about sin. They engraved lines about idolatry. They pressed into their children's hearts the ways of a wicked world.

These adults did not write with pencil, but with iron. It's not a sharpie but a diamond point. They didn't write on their bedroom walls, but on the sides of their hearts.

They wrote by their example. The children knew of the false altars, the pagan gods, the sacred poles. They saw the ritual sexual rites. They witnessed other children burned on the altars. These parents taught their children the wrong things.

What's the answer, Jeremiah? Are there other options? Jeremiah revealed the answer in one of his prayers. He called them to teach. "I will make them know" the power and might of God (Jer. 16:21). They would be taught the name of the LORD.

God called for instruction. That should come as no surprise. It's been that way since the beginning. Teaching is at the heart of what we believe. Moses told Israel to teach their children diligently (Deut. 6:7), the psalmist reminds us God's Word is like a lamp (Ps. 119:105), and Jesus left us with the command to go everywhere and "preach the gospel" (Mark 16:15). Paul instructed Timothy to instruct others (2 Tim. 2:2), and we're reminded that "all Scripture is inspired by God and profitable" in many ways (2 Tim. 3:16–17). The call to teach reverberates throughout the Bible.

In the midst of terrible times in ancient Jerusalem, with violence on the streets, when the corpses of children rotted along the road, Jeremiah didn't call for a better school system. He didn't call for a rally on the national mall in Jerusalem. He didn't initiate a letter-writing campaign to the king. All that may be good, but it was not what Jeremiah urged. In a sense, it wasn't what was best.

He called them to teach the children the might and power of God.

Most people remember Dwight Moody as one of the most remarkable preachers in America. He died in 1899. While working in a shoe store in Boston, he started to follow Jesus. Later, he spent much of his time trying to teach children in Chicago about God. He taught them about the power and might of God, and what he taught them changed the city.

Moody tells of trying to get the son of the owner of a neighborhood bar to come to church. Afraid to go into the bar, Moody paced the sidewalk. He worried that if he went into the bar to evangelize, people would think he was inside drinking. Finally, he looked in both directions and went in.

The boy's father looked up, saw the preacher, and cried out, "We don't have any preaching hypocrites here." The frightened Moody fled.

Moody returned. The bar owner cried out, "I'd rather have my sons drunkards and my daughters harlots than to have them Christians." Moody persevered. He challenged the bar owner to a reading challenge. Moody agreed to read Thomas Paine's *Age of Reason* at the owner's insistence, and in turn Moody asked him to read the *New Testament*. As they got to know each other, Moody invited the bar owner to church. The owner said, "I haven't been to church in eighteen years. No, I won't go. But you can have church here if you want to."

Initially appalled at the idea of church in a bar, Moody considered it and finally agreed. The bar owner said, "You can preach for fifteen minutes, and then I get to talk the rest of the hour." When they met that day, Moody brought a young boy he had worked with in his ministry. Moody preached fifteen minutes. The bar owner talked forty-five.

Then Moody asked the young boy to pray. With a soft voice, the child asked God to forgive the man for talking against Jesus. Then a strange thing happened. One by one, the men who had made fun of Moody left the bar. Finally, the three remained: the owner, Moody, and the boy.

The bar owner said, "If that is what you teach your children, you can have mine."[2]

Things have not changed much. The wicked world of Jeremiah's day, the depraved times of Dwight Moody, and the contemporary world of Body Count continue their way.

We respond by engraving a child's heart with the power and might of God. Better schools will also help. More police will make things better. Safer streets will benefit all.

But nothing comes close to engraving a child's heart with the Word of God.

Continuities. I suspect in the minds of many Christians, and certainly in the public worship of many congregations, there is dissatisfaction

---

[2] Bonnie C. Harvey, *D. L. Moody: The American Evangelist* (Uhrichsville, OH: Barbour & Company, 1997), 55–57.

with the way our culture is drifting from God. We are appalled at the lyrics of music, the content of videos, the laws of our legislatures, and the practices of our fellow citizens. This oppressive culture hurts the children. Do we hear their cries? Do we see the gospel as the solution to the dissatisfactions we have with culture? If we speak the gospel to the vulnerable, are we willing to make room for those who respond?

WHAT DO YOU THINK?

1. Where do children in your community learn about drugs, violence, and sin? Give examples.

2. Who is responsible in your community for teaching right and wrong and the standards of God? How effective are those teachers?

3. Do Christians believe that teaching God's Word can change the world? Give evidence for your answer.

4. What churches in your community are engaged with the lives of children and teens? How are they involved? Is this making a difference? Explain.

14

A TIME OF REVIVAL—
THE JEPHTHAH STORY

JUDGES 10-12

Most people don't like the Jephthah story. Nobody lives happily ever after. We don't tell our children this story in Sunday school. No church advertises its VBS as "Come be a Jephthah." Most preachers avoid it.

Two people did dwell on the Jephthah story. Samuel referred to Jephthah in his farewell speech in 1 Samuel 12:11. He reminded us that God always sends leaders. The author of the book of Hebrews is the other who reflected on Jephthah. Hebrews 11 lists people of faith and included Jephthah along with Abraham, Noah, and Moses.

1 Samuel 12 and Hebrews 11 remind us of two great biblical themes: *One is that God's people do not always do what he wants.* For example, after Deuteronomy tells what God expects, the book of Joshua shares stories of people doing right, but then the book of Judges tells of people not doing right. Joshua reveals that even in good times, there are bad people, while Judges states the opposite: that even in bad times, there are good people. Exodus 34:5–7 reminds us that when people do not do what God wants, the effects last for generations.

The second great biblical theme is that God gives grace. In Deuteronomy and Joshua, he gave people the land; in Judges, he sent his Spirit. His mercy cannot be depleted. His patience is remarkable. He gives grace to the most flawed people, including people like Jephthah.

We live and work in that world. A parent sins and the child suffers, but God provides grace. Good people do bad things and others pay the price, but God stands ready to redeem. We live among flawed people under the watchful eye of a grace-filled God.

The Jephthah story is complicated. It opens in Judges 10 with the report of Israel doing evil in the sight of the LORD. God responded by sending the Ammonites to oppress Israel. Even though Israel cried out to God, he resisted, questioning their loyalty and telling them to ask their idols to rescue them. But eventually, God again intervened on Israel's behalf.

The story centers in a place called Gilead, located east of the Jordan River. This area is far from the core of Israel on the west side. The west side is the home of the famous cities of Hebron, Bethlehem, Jerusalem, Shiloh, and Shechem. Gilead is on the east side of the Jordan—the home of lesser-known places. Gilead is Israel, but not real Israel. It's across the tracks, on the other side of town. Some might call it a bad neighborhood.

Judges 11:1–3 provides a brief flashback. An unnamed prostitute bore a son named Jephthah. His name means "opening" (that becomes important later). His father, Gilead, claimed the boy and appeared to include him in the family will. Other sons of Gilead refused to share the inheritance, and they kicked Jephthah out of town. He became the leader of a gang of worthless men far from home. What do we make of Jephthah?

In short, Jephthah was an abandoned child. Perhaps the harlot mother didn't know which man the father was, so she claimed the father was Gilead. At first read, it appears Gilead is a man, but since the term most often referred to the nation or the region, Gilead could refer to the men of Gilead who used the services of Jephthah's mother.

Jephthah was an unwanted child. His mother worked at night. His father's family didn't want him. Other kids knew the circumstances of his birth, so Jephthah learned to take care of himself, how to be hard, and how to lead. He fell into a gang that seemed to involve crime and violence to the point that they avoided civilized society. Jephthah had no direction, no focus, no morality, and no committed relationships.

His story sounds familiar. An unwanted child from a dysfunctional family turns to crime, makes friends with other dysfunctional youths, and participates in violence. We know some contemporary Jephthahs. We know his face. We hear his story.

The Ammonite oppression grew so strong that community leaders needed an expert in violence and leadership, somebody with nothing to lose. Why should they send their sons into battle when they could call on Jephthah? Who would cry if Jephthah died in the line of duty? Jephthah got what he wanted from the leaders of Gilead. They gave him command of the army and the headship of the people.

We know this man. We know the young men who become con artists, who can talk their way out of any situation, who can bargain and manipulate, who are survivors, and who know how to cope. In the end, Jephthah received what he wanted. He got accepted by the people who rejected him. In the end, the leaders got what they wanted, somebody they could risk losing.

As the new leader of Gilead, Jephthah tried to talk his way out of a fight with Ammon. Despite Jephthah's long speech in Judges 11:12–28, the Ammonite king basically said, "No comment," and readied for battle.

As the battle line formed, the Spirit of the LORD came upon Jephthah (Judg. 11:29). The broad understanding of this line that appears seven times in the book of Judges on the most unworthy of people suggests that God chose a person who could deliver his people and that he, the LORD, guaranteed the victory.

Whether Jephthah knew about the Spirit of the LORD is unclear. What is clear is that he continued to be Jephthah. He now sought to make arrangements with the LORD. If God gave him the victory over Ammon, when he returned, he vowed to offer as a sacrifice the first person who came out of the house (Judg. 11:31). The language here could refer to an animal. Jephthah used the masculine singular five times to refer to his offering.

Jephthah led the army of Gilead to a decisive victory over the Ammonites. Upon his return, the one who opened the door of the house of the man whose name means "opening" was his only daughter. Astounded at the terrible end of his vow, Jephthah tore his clothes and blamed his daughter for giving him trouble. She asked for two months to grieve over her virginity. When she returned, Jephthah fulfilled his vow (Judg. 11:34–40).

The story tells of three generations. Generation one includes a nameless harlot and an ambiguous father. Generation two is the rejected Jephthah, who became an orphan, gang member, violent youth, and a con artist. Generation three is Jephthah's daughter. She is another nameless woman with no mother to protect her and no community to rise up in her defense. Three times the text says she is a virgin. There is no generation four.

We want to know why the story ends this way. We want to explain away the child sacrifice. God hates human sacrifice. Why did the writer of Hebrews include such a man in his listing of the faithful?

The story underlines the destiny of those who do not do what God wants. The effects can last generations. God knows the cost of human sin.

But we wonder why this story is in Judges. What do we learn about listening from this rash young man?

The Jephthah story is about people who did not listen. It's about a community that remained silent and ignored what was happening around them. The men of Gilead slept with the harlot. One of them fathered Jephthah. Others disowned him and sent him away. Nobody in Gilead put a stop to the harlot's work. Nobody spoke up for young Jephthah. Only later did the opportunistic leaders of Gilead send for Jephthah to be their chief. He led their army to victory. He returned in triumph. He ended the oppression.

The community continued its silence. Nobody in Mizpah spoke or acted or advocated for Jephthah. Nobody counseled Jephthah about his vow. Nobody told Jephthah about Leviticus 5:4–13 or 27:1–8, which described how to back out of a vow. Jephthah did not know, perhaps because the people who studied the law of Moses with the children didn't want their children to rub shoulders with the likes of Jephthah. After all, his mother was a harlot.

It would have been a simple matter. "Jephthah, you can back out of the vow. There's a cost to backing out, but violating a vow pales in comparison to human sacrifice." But nobody said a word.

Jephthah planned to burn his daughter as a sacrifice. He agreed for her to spend two months with her friends before the offering. Nobody in Gilead made any move during those two months to change the outcome. Nobody came to her aid.

Then came the day when Jephthah tied up his daughter and headed for the town altar. Nobody said a word. None of the older people offered advice. Nobody offered a different path. No one said, "Jephthah, untie those ropes." As the odor of roasting flesh drifted through the small town of Mizpah, nobody intervened.

The community that thrust out Jephthah, who hired him to save their town, remained silent as this young father committed a great wrong. They celebrated his victory, but ignored his failure as a father.

We want to know more, but there is no more. The fact is, Jephthah killed his little girl by sacrificing her on the altar. Nobody stopped him. Not a single person. Nobody.

Fathers continue to kill their children in our own day. Nobody stops them. Not a single person. Nobody.

Continuities. Do you hear the cries of the contemporary children being violated, abused, and killed in the city where you live? Do you feel any responsibility at all to make room?

WHAT DO YOU THINK?

1. What troubles you about the Jephthah story?

2. Evaluate the comparison between Jephthah and today's discarded youth.

3. What efforts are made to redirect the vulnerable youth in your community?

4. Why do you believe Jephthah is listed as a person of faith in Hebrews 11?

15

BALANCING SPIRITUAL PORTFOLIOS

JOHN 10:10-11

Balancing the books is a central concern in the business world, whether it's the New York Stock Exchange or the local privately held retail store. Most businesses can't survive if they don't match revenue with expenses.

Balancing one's spiritual portfolio can be just as significant. Whether we think about vulnerable children or consider our own spiritual bottom line, raising our human value can be a significant piece of our spiritual health.

I have vivid memories of standing at the corner of U.S. Highway 422 and Gates Avenue in a small town in western Pennsylvania. I grew up on Gates Avenue near the corner where our street met the major highway. This corner was where I could wait on rides. Someone would pick me up for a youth group activity, or my summer boss would stop early in the morning to give me a ride to the potato farm.

I recall arranging to go to a particular church event. My parents did not go to church, so before I could drive, I had to depend on people from church for a ride. An adult agreed to pick me up at my corner. I arrived ten minutes early, watched the traffic, then looked for that adult's car. I waited thirty minutes and started to think he was really late. After forty-five minutes, I began to think he wasn't coming at all. When my watch reached an hour, I walked home and told my parents I had been forgotten. The adult who promised to pick me up didn't remember. He didn't remember, but

I did. I still remember how troubled I felt. Standing alone at the corner for somebody who wasn't coming made me feel like a nobody, unwanted and vulnerable.

It's a common feeling. We all wait at life's corners for people who have forgotten us. Experiences like that make us think we are unwanted and vulnerable. We all have our corners that make us think we have no value.

Yet, I distinctly remember that at the same time I had that corner experience, I learned about another image. I learned about this image at church. In fact, the first verse I ever memorized was about this image. It was the image of a shepherd.

The verse was John 10:11: "I am the good shepherd. The good shepherd lays down his life for the sheep." Jesus says it three times, "I am the good shepherd." He promises his sheep abundant life. He knows the names of all his sheep. All his sheep know the sound of his voice.

I remember how much that helped me. When I felt forgotten at my corner, I thought, "Jesus has not forgotten me, because he knows my name." When I felt alone at my corner, I thought, "But Jesus is with me, because he never leaves his sheep alone." When I felt like a nobody at my corner, I thought, "But Jesus gave me abundant life, so I must be somebody."

I didn't grow up on a farm. I met my first shepherd when I was thirty. Yet even as a city kid, I understood this image. Maybe Jesus chose this image because it is so easy to understand. The shepherd protects his sheep. He spends so much time with them that he knows their names, and they know the sound of his voice. My two experiences with sheep verified those truths.

As a college student, I lived a semester in Herzliya, Israel. It was a suburb of Tel Aviv filled with high-rise apartments, buses, shopping, and parking lots. My bedroom was a closed-in balcony on the fourth floor flat. Every morning, a shepherd would lead his flock beneath my window. I thought it was strange seeing sheep in the city. I could see cars, streets, high-rise buildings, and then this flock of sheep. Despite the distractions, the sheep followed their shepherd through the city maze.

My other experience came when I took my family to Gene's farm in western Iowa. Highway 44 cut between the farmhouse and the barn. After church one Sunday night, we went to the farm with Gene. He stood at the barn and started calling names. Fuzzy. Buzz. Woolly. Sparky. I couldn't see a single sheep. There were no animals in sight.

Suddenly, all I could hear was "Baa. Baa." A whole flock of sheep ran over the top of the hill toward Gene. Then they stopped and refused to come closer. They knew Gene but did not know us.

I learned from Gene the difference between a cowboy and a shepherd. A cowboy drives the herd. The shepherd leads the flock. The cowboy throws a lasso around the cow's neck. The shepherd uses a staff to guide and direct. The cowboy cracks a whip. The shepherd calls the sheep by name.

Lynn Anderson in his book *They Smell Like Sheep* tells of a man named Roy who was traveling through a rural part of the Middle East. When they came to the top of a ridge, they looked down into the valley. The narrow part of the valley opened at one end to a large green pasture. He could see how the single trail through the narrow part of the valley became several branch trails that went through the large pasture.

Roy watched six different shepherds walking together down the narrow part of the valley. Sheep surrounded them on each side. Finally, they came to the place where one path forked into the several paths. The shepherds said goodbye to each other, and each shepherd took a separate path. Then an amazing thing happened. As the shepherds separated, so did the sheep. Each flock followed its own shepherd. As the six shepherds moved onto their own path, they each stopped and looked back for strays. One by one, the six shepherds cupped their hands over their mouths and cried out. The strays looked up, heard a distinct voice, and ran after their shepherd.[1]

My mother suffers from Alzheimer's. When the disease first started to display its effects, her short-term memory faded. She could remember that she couldn't remember. She regularly told me, "I don't remember very well." We lived in Memphis; she lived in Phoenix. I would call regularly. Every time the phone rang, Mom answered, and I'd say, "Hello, Mom."

The next line, every single time, was "Hello, Harold." Despite all the things she had forgotten, she remembered my voice. She knew my name.

---

[1] Lynn Anderson, *They Smell Like Sheep* (West Monroe: Howard Publishing Company, 1997), 15–16.

Those days have now passed. But I remember how important it was that she remembered my name. Even though my mother does not now remember me at all, I still have somebody that knows my name.

We all have our corners where we feel forgotten. Sometimes it seems like nobody cares and that we're not important to anyone. But there is someone who always knows us. He's the Good Shepherd. He always knows your name.

Continuities. Jesus knows when his sheep cry out. He is listening. Are we?

WHAT DO YOU THINK?

1. Tell about a time in your life when you felt left out and forgotten. Why do these memories remain so strong throughout our lives?

2. Describe an experience with sheep. How does this help you to understand Jesus's interest in us?

3. How does being forgotten and never knowing about Jesus affect the lives of vulnerable children?

4. Besides the shepherd knowing your name, what are other ways we can know we are valuable to God from Scripture?

16

BIRTHRIGHT— BURDEN OF THE PAST

MARK 10:45; LUKE 6:36, 19:10

With a full plate of food in hand, I looked for a place to sit at the church potluck. I spied two empty seats. One open chair was next to a visiting family with four little children. I noticed scraps of food all over the table despite the parents' efforts to keep the meal in order. The father stuttered. The mother appeared a bit unkempt. The children seemed out of control.

The second empty seat was to the right of a person of some fame in our community. He was known by many people as a great personality and fun to be around, and I found it amazing that nobody had taken the strategic spot.

As I balanced my chicken and green beans, I had a moment to decide. I sat by the man of some fame.

On another occasion, I recall leaving church one Sunday morning only to encounter two people. A widower stopped me to ask a question. I couldn't understand his shaky voice, and his question didn't make sense. As we spoke, I noticed a preacher from another congregation. Well known among local leaders, most considered him to be a mover and shaker in the community.

I ended the conversation with the old man and engaged the famous preacher.

Beverly and Jerry make a striking couple. Gregarious, dashingly good looking, vivacious, they make friends easily. Brandon, another friend of mine, tells of having his morning coffee at a local shop when a disabled man with unattractive features and offensive habits entered. Brandon knew the man and didn't want to be seen with him, so left to avoid the encounter.

Later that week, Beverly and Jerry asked Brandon if he had seen this disabled man whom they both knew. Brandon asked Beverly why she wanted to know. She said, "Jerry and I want to invite him over for Christmas dinner."

We all know these feelings. We feel attracted to the handsome, the powerful, the wealthy. We avoid those who lack admirable qualities. We seek out those who stand above us on life's ladder and avoid the ones below. Few of us are like Jerry and Beverly. Why do we act the way we do?

It comes with our society. We find ourselves prisoners of the rules of culture. We follow the scripts we learned as children. Cater to the powerful, sit by the wealthy, attend to the famous, associate with the pretty or the handsome.

God moves in the opposite direction. Remember the story in Genesis 25. Rebekah was expecting twins. Isaac prepared to follow the dictates of his time. The firstborn got the honor, the money, the status, the influence. Esau received the silver spoon. Looking ahead, it might make sense. The younger of the two brothers had conflict with almost everybody he met, and he would grow up to deceive his father and his father-in-law. Eventually, he would wrestle even God.

God did an amazing thing. Against the rules of society, against the script of the ancient world, against all culture, he chose to side with Jacob.

When we start thinking about God's preference for the underdog, the second-born, the vulnerable, we find it everywhere.

To establish God's own nation, he passed by Nimrod and Nebuchadnezzar and picked Abram. He didn't call the Egyptians or the Hittites to special blessing, but Israel. He nominated the youngest, smallest son of Jesse to be king, not David's more powerful brothers. Jesus's disciples did not include wealthy Romans or powerful Greeks, but Galilean fishermen. He chose a tax collector, not a businessman along the Appian Way.

The silver spoon does not sway God. Moses described God as "God of gods and the Lord of lords, the great, the mighty, and the terrible God" (Deut. 10:17). Then in the same breath he continued, "He executes justice for the fatherless and the widow, and loves the sojourner" (Deut. 10:18). Isn't that just like God to include the outcast? In one of the most majestic pictures of God anywhere in the Bible, God stands next to the orphans, widows, and aliens.

In Matthew 19:16, a young, wealthy, well-placed member of society came to see Jesus. He had the silver spoon. Jesus challenged him. The man left disappointed. Jesus turned to the crowd to note that the first will be last and the last will be first.

Paul put it succinctly: God picks the low and despised in the world because his foolishness trumps human wisdom every day of the week (1 Cor. 1:25–28). Why does God work this way? Three verses tell us why:

First, "Be merciful, even as your Father is merciful" (Luke 6:36). Mercy trumps local culture every time. It made God line up alongside the orphan, widow, and alien. Those who follow Jesus form the line the same way. Create a heart of mercy.

Second, "For the Son of man also came not to be served, but to serve" (Mark 10:45). The cash flow of culture says do what makes the most profit. God came with the countercultural point of view. Jesus and the people like him look for ways to stand at the end of the line and help those who struggle to find the line.

Third, "For the Son of man came to seek and to save the lost" (Luke 19:10). God reaches out to those who are the furthest away from him. Being at one with God counters our most cherished traditions and rewrites our deeply learned scripts.

Most of us take a lifetime to learn these lessons. It reminds me of Billy of the Impact Church in Houston. Ron Sellers, one of the ministers at Impact, told me about Billy. He constantly brought people to this inner-city church. He told them about Jesus. Billy demonstrated to his friends how Jesus regularly reached down the ladder to pull others up.

Then came a hot day in August 1995 when two cars collided on the Southwest Freeway. Arriving on the scene before anybody else, Billy discovered a young woman pinned in her car. He managed to pull her out of the car. He was about to carry her to safety. Just then, another car came over the crest of the hill on the freeway. Intoxicated, the driver aimed his car directly at them. Billy pushed the injured girl toward the median. He turned around, and his body took the full impact of the car. Billy died at the scene.

Not many attended the funeral. Billy was not famous or rich or powerful. Doug Williams told the story of Billy's last actions. He said, "In that moment, Billy was all that he ever wanted to be. He did as Jesus had done for him. In so doing, his Father enabled him to save an angel."

Then Doug introduced a woman in a wheelchair. It was the girl Billy had died to save.

Continuities. Places like Gus's Bar and Grill, or James Kinney's group of six men around a fire, or the gang violence in Los Angeles characterized by the boy named Body Count all remind us of the vulnerable people all around us. If we follow God's mission, we listen to their voices. We listen to contemporary youths like Jephthah, and the child forgotten at their corner, or a homeless man like Billy before he died on a Houston freeway. They represent voices we must hear—voices that we normally do not hear. We find it easier to pass them by at the church potluck or avoid having them over to the house, but the vulnerable people of our world face the pain of their brokenness. When we join God on his mission to fix the broken world, we move to within earshot of their voices.

The next chapters consider the means God uses to fix their brokenness. When we or these vulnerable people feel blessed and valued, have a sense of being at home, and know that God values and cares, God does his work of fixing their broken world.

WHAT DO YOU THINK?

1. Give examples of people (including you) catering to those above them and ignoring those below them.

2. Jesus came to show mercy, be a servant, and to save the lost. Christians are to be like him. Which of those qualities do you find easiest to imitate? Which of the three qualities is the hardest for you to imitate?

3. What did you think when you read Billy's story? How are you like him or different from him?

4. Besides the examples the author uses, who in Scripture does God choose and use for his purposes and glory that others would call useless, unattractive, common, or the underdog?

PART 3

LISTENING TO GOD ABOUT CHILDREN

When we listen to the cries of the world's vulnerable people, we learn there are many "not goods" in God's "good" world, too many "not okays," too many Jephthahs, too much loneliness, and too much pain. Really listening to those voices has a profound effect on us.

We also must listen to God. It's his mission that we take up. He made the good world. We broke it. He came to fix it. He enlists us on his fix-it team to work with him to restore his world.

Many of us are successful Americans. Often, we believe our American ingenuity must be applied to these situations. There's no doubt some truth there. But before we run out to solve all these problems, we must listen to what God says about these vulnerable people and what he thinks they need. In order to do that, we must go back to the beginning. How did God intend for the world to operate?

17

BLESSING— BLUEPRINT FOR THE FUTURE

HEBREWS 11:20-21

Every year, schoolteachers have a week of meetings and training sessions to give instructors orientation and inspiration. Some years ago, at many such gatherings, administrators showed a film entitled *A Cipher in the Snow*. An Idaho schoolteacher and school counselor, Jean Mizer, wrote it and published it in the *National Education Association Journal* in 1964. Later, it appeared as a short movie.

It opened with a group of children waiting for the school bus. They lived in a rural area and waited for the bus on a cold winter morning. Most of the children enjoyed the snow and each other.

Except for Cliff. He stood alone. The other children ran by him. They ignored him.

When the bus arrived, the children all crowded to get on, except Cliff, who hung back. The students happily took a seat with their friends, except for Cliff, who sat by himself behind the driver. Everyone chattered, except for Cliff, who spoke to no one.

As the bus lumbered down the snow-covered road, Cliff suddenly dropped his books and staggered to his feet. The driver saw him in the rearview mirror.

"What's the matter, kid? Are you sick?"

Cliff asked to be let off. The driver pulled over and opened the door. Cliff pitched forward and fell into the snow.

As the movie ended, a siren sounded while the driver stood over Cliff's body. It was too late. Cliff was dead.

The movie inferred that Cliff was in good health. As it went on, it became clear that Cliff was an ostracized student. After his parents' divorce, he withdrew. His math teacher learned that he was Cliff's favorite instructor. He had no idea. The school asked him to notify the parents and write an obituary. He tried to enlist others to go to the funeral. Barely ten people even knew Cliff.

The movie maintained that Cliff died from a broken heart. He was alone. He was a nobody. He was a zero. He was a cipher in the snow.

Cliff represents many children in America—those who have no parents or whose parents are there physically but not emotionally, or whose parents are more interested in their career than their children. He symbolizes children whose parents are so involved in their own lives that they have nothing to give to their children. He represents those teens with imprisoned fathers and dope-ridden mothers. Cliff gives a name to the abused and bullied and alone.

Cliff's story raises a host of questions in our minds. What's wrong here? How can such an advanced nation as ours continually produce children like Cliff? Do we know how to address these problems? What should we do?

The book of Genesis speaks extensively about children. Cain and Abel are the first children. Noah takes his three sons into the ark. Abraham and Sarah wait for a promised child. Isaac and Rebekah have twins. Jacob becomes the father of a dozen boys and one daughter. One of the closing scenes has grandfather Jacob blessing his two grandsons. Genesis celebrates children.

Yet even in Genesis, not all children do well. Cain kills his brother Abel. Genesis 4 talks about child abuse. Abraham tells his first son to leave home. Joseph's brothers sell him into slavery.

One significant word turns up repeatedly in the Genesis discussion about children. It's the word *blessing*. Most people skim over the word. Think about how we use this word. We equate it with the prayer for the food. We bless people when they sneeze. Or when somebody does something incredibly stupid, we say, "Bless his little heart."

Yet blessing is a weighty theological concept. Blessing means somebody significant planning the best for another person. In some ways, blessing carries the idea that people are valuable, important, and significant. It means that those blessed should have the best that life has to offer.

Genesis tells of children constantly being blessed. After the flood, God blessed Noah and his sons (9:1). God promised to bless all of Abraham's children (12:2). Even the discarded son, Ishmael, received a blessing (17:20). Laban blessed his grandchildren (31:55).

Two striking cases draw our attention. In Genesis 27, Isaac prepared to bless Esau. His wife Rebekah and his other son Jacob schemed to deceive the blind father. Instead of blessing Esau, he blessed Jacob. When Esau pled for blessing, Isaac blessed him too. This story tells of one of the Bible's first dysfunctional families. They needed counseling. But in the midst of the chaos, both boys got a blessing.

In Genesis 48, Joseph asked his father Jacob to bless his sons Ephraim and Manasseh. He put the older boy, Manasseh, on his father's right, which at that time meant he would receive the primary blessing. Ephraim stood on his grandfather's left. When time came to bless the boys, scheming Jacob crossed his hands and gave the younger son, Ephraim, the primary blessing. Even today, we commonly say Ephraim and Manasseh, putting the younger son first.

Genesis offers no rigid formula for passing on the blessing. We see touching, speaking, and the intention to give their offspring the best they have to offer. Yet despite the lack of an inspired formula, we know when the blessing has been passed on.

In Jay Leno's *Leading with My Chin,* he tells of saving up enough money in high school to buy an old pickup truck. He worked on it all the time. He took pride in installing new upholstery in the cab. Later, he accidently broke one of the cab's windows, but didn't have enough money to get it fixed.

He drove the truck to high school and left it in student parking. One day in class, he looked out the classroom window to see a storm moving in. It started to rain. He feared the rain would ruin his upholstery. Then he saw the family car pull into the lot, stop behind his pickup, and his parents pop out. They took a piece of plastic and covered the broken window. He realized they had seen the storm, knew about the window, left work, and saved the day.

Jay Leno said he sat in class and cried.[1]

Bud Greenspan made movies about remarkable events at the Olympic Games. One involved Bill Havens, whom many hoped would win a gold medal for rowing for America in the 1924 games. Before the games, his wife was expecting their first child. As it turned out, the date of the birth and the Olympics overlapped. Bill gave up his chance for the gold to be at his wife's bedside when their son Frank was born. He was never sure he made the right decision.

In 1952, Bill received a telegraph from the Olympic Games. It said,

"Dear Dad, Thanks for waiting around for me to get born in 1924. I'm coming home with the gold medal you should have won."

It was signed, "Your loving son, Frank."

Frank Havens won the gold medal in the solo 10,000-meter canoeing event, the same event his father would have entered in 1924.[2]

We see the common thread in both stories is the blessing. Both boys had parents who cared. Both had significant adults in their lives who considered them valuable and important.

We can be grateful for the Jay Lenos and Frank Havens of the world. But what about the Cliffs? What about the children who don't have parents who care? What about those who nobody seems to value?

The answer lies in the book of Genesis. The opening chapter describes six creative days. God made the world, light, land, vegetation, the planets, birds, fish, and land animals. Then, at the height of creation, he formed humanity.

After creating humans, God did something remarkable. He blessed them. He considered them valuable and important and significant.

[1] Jay Leno, *Leading with My Chin* (New York: Harper Paperbacks, 1996), 50.
[2] Bud Greenspan, *Golden Moments in U.S. Olympic History* (Baarn, Netherlands: Polygram Video, 1996).

In the next ten chapters (Gen. 2–11), the people undid the blessing. What God considered valuable, they treated as valueless. What God held as worthwhile, they treated as worthless. Murder, abuse, violence, and selfishness reign. Then comes Genesis 12. God in effect slammed his fist on the table and shouted, "No! No! That's not the way it's supposed to be." Then he blessed Abraham and instructed Abraham to spread the blessing to the entire world.

How does blessing spread? How do people get the affirmation of being valued and worthwhile? Go back to Genesis 1.

All of the created things are called good. Light and water and birds and fish all get evaluated as good. God made them all good. All of them are a blessing, but none of these items God created can pass on the blessing. Light can't pass on the blessing. Water can't bless a child. Birds and fish can't make a youngster feel valued.

Only one creature in Genesis 1 is made like God, with the ability to pass on the blessing. That one creature is you.

Continuities. If I were pressed to give one biblical truth missing in most of our churches, I would point to the one about blessing. We talk about blessing, but not in the biblical sense. We practice blessing ourselves and those we love, but we do not reflect seriously on how the people of God bless the community around them, much less the vulnerable people of our world. Surely the people of God ought to be the ones who treat others as people made in the image of God who have value, significance, and worth.

WHAT DO YOU THINK?

1. Do you feel valued and significant? If you do, how did you come to sense your own worthiness? If you do not, how do you think things might have been different?

2. What child or adult do you know who appears to have little sense of their own value? How do their actions reflect their own sense of unworthiness?

3. List ways in which a congregation could bless the children of Christians. Think of ways in which a congregation could bless the children who live near the church building.

4. Our society talks a great deal about giving children self-worth. How is this the same or different from blessing?

18

THE ASKED-FOR CHILD

1 SAMUEL 1:26-28

Sally and I visited Sheffield Elementary School in Memphis, Tennessee, in the fall of 2017. We found eight hundred children in a structure built for four hundred students. Most of the children came from disadvantaged families. About a third of the students were Hispanic, and they spoke seven dialects of Spanish. Many of the students did not know English.

The principal had a doctorate in education. She asked her supervisors to transfer her to this school so she could make a difference. Every year she had been there, the school board cut the budget and sent her more children.

She told us about a mother who was in her office that morning. Frustrated with her third-grade child, the mother shouted, "I can't do anything with her. I don't want her anymore. You take her." The mother stomped out of the office and left her crying daughter with the principal.

I don't know what it feels like to be a third grader whom nobody wants. I do know there are thousands like her in American cities and in other nations around the world. I know that some get sold as sex slaves, others are ignored by their teacher, and most never learn to read well. Often, they end up on drugs or on public assistance or in prison. The stories are overwhelming.

The number of unwanted children in the world defies belief. The masses of people who feel undesirable staggers the imagination. "I don't want her anymore. You take her."

Somebody put a post on the web. It had these lines: "I'm the ugly sister. I'm the horrible daughter. I'm not even second choice. I'm the 'leftover.' I'm the not clever one. I'm the not skinny one. I'm the talentless one. I'm the 'why are you even here?' one."

On the surface, the scene in 1 Samuel 1–2 sounds like our time. One of the main characters is a man. He had more than one woman. He came from a nondescript family. One of his women couldn't have children. He didn't understand her, at times berated her, and treated her unfairly.

There are two women in the story. The one woman who might have comforted the barren woman offered little help. Instead, she put her down. The family fought and tore at each other. Since the troubled woman had little support at home, she decided to try the spiritual community. She ended up at the door of the temple praying. The preacher-type thought she was drunk, and he started to berate her too. Several children appear in the story. One was raised in a foster home situation.

That's the story of Hannah on the surface; but when we dig deeper, we find another narrative. It unfolds in five scenes.

Scene one comes in 1 Samuel 1:3–8, which describes the problem. Hannah can't have a baby. The family was filled with dysfunction. She was unhappy, seemingly depressed, and refused to eat. The husband was unable to solve the problem.

Scene two in 1 Samuel 1:9–18 tells the complaint. Hannah went to the tabernacle to pray. Verse 10 says she was deeply distressed and wept bitterly. In her pain, she offered God a proposal. *You give me a son, and I'll give him back to you.* Then the priest Eli noticed Hannah and misinterpreted her distress as drunkenness. After a brief conversation, he gave her a blessing.

Scene three in 1 Samuel 1:19–20 gives the solution. Hannah was pregnant! She let everybody know!

Scene four comes in 1 Samuel 1:21–28, which describes thanksgiving. Hannah said, "For this child I prayed; and the LORD has granted me my petition which I made to him. Therefore I have lent him to the LORD; as long as he lives, he is lent to the LORD" (1 Sam. 1:27–28).

The Hebrew word *sha'al* appears seven times in this chapter. It means "to ask for." Eli used it twice.[1] He told Hannah that he hoped God would give

---

[1] The Hebrew *sha'al* stands behind "petition" and "made" in 1 Samuel 1:17.

her what she asks. In verse 20, when Hannah learned she was expecting a baby, she said, "This child is what I asked for." When she presented the baby to God in the presence of Eli in verse 27, she used the word twice.[2] "God gave me what I asked for." Then, as Hannah planned the child's future in verse 28, she used the same word twice again. This child, the asked-for child, belonged to God. Some Bible versions translate the word as "lent."

This story is about the "asked for" child, not the "I don't want you anymore" child. Not the "you take her" child. Not the "let's sell our daughter into the sex trade because we need the money" child. Not the "get out of here, you're messing up my life" child. Not the "let's abort this" child. Not the "I don't love you anymore" child. This child is the "asked for" child.

During a summer ministry internship while I was in college, I lived with a family that thought of me as their own son. Jim and Jo treated me with hospitality and respect. Later, I became a missionary of that congregation. Some problems developed, and I was called back to the home church to explain our actions before all the men of the congregation. Jim was a factory worker, not a verbal man. But in that meeting, he stood up. He was in the back. I was at the front in the spotlight. Jim looked at me and said, "Harold, I used to love you as a son, but I don't love you anymore."

"I can't do anything with her. I don't want her anymore. You take her."

The asked-for child. The wanted child. The loved child.

What does all this reflection on the asked-for child mean? Here are two thoughts.

First, some of us have been the unwanted child. We know the rejection and pain. We understand the isolation and the vulnerability. Some of us act out our "unwantedness" with alcohol or promiscuity or offensive behavior. We respond to being unwanted with depression or hurting ourselves and others.

The story of Hannah reminds us of the importance of being wanted. When Eli blessed Hannah at the temple, it changed everything. It reminds us that God wants all those unwanted children. You and I may feel unwanted, but God wants us.

---

[2] *Sha'al* appears in the RSV of 1 Samuel 1:27 as "petition" and "asked."

Second, all of us must become like Hannah. We must be the ones to say, "I want this child." We must believe that our own children are the asked-for children. We must ensure that the children at church and the ones in the neighborhood are the asked-for children.

There's one more scene in the story. Scene five comes in 1 Samuel 2:1–10. It's Hannah's song that she sang after the asked-for baby was given back to God. After Mary had Jesus in the New Testament, she sang a song with similar words.

The song has two points: One point stresses God's power. There is nobody as holy and as solid as our God. The other point is that God does the unexpected. He raises up the poor from the dust and the needy from the trash pile to make them sit in places of honor. He is the God who wants us all.

The name of Hannah's little boy is Samuel. He grew up to become the great prophet of God. He anointed the first two kings of Israel. God took a boy from a dysfunctional home and made him rub shoulders with the great. According to 1 Samuel 1:20, Samuel's name has a meaning.

It means "asked for by God."

Continuities. This book on listening and making room has roots in over two decades of instruction and encouragement to women and men working in Christian child care. They call themselves Network 1:27. The name comes from three biblical verses about children. We'll investigate all three in this book. One of the three verses is 1 Samuel 1:27. These good people who work on the front lines with vulnerable children believe every child should be "asked for."

WHAT DO YOU THINK?

1. Tell about a child you know who appears to be unwanted. Why are children unwanted?

2. Describe a time when you felt unwanted. What are the effects of feeling unwanted?

3. What key elements in the story point to Samuel being the "wanted child"?

4. How can local congregations help children feel wanted?

5. Reread Hannah's song in 1 Samuel 2:1–10. Is the focus of her song what you expect? Why or why not?

6. Think of a child you know that is unwanted. What can you do this week to help that child feel wanted?

19

READY

LUKE 15:20

My parents once owned a small farm in western Pennsylvania nestled between two Appalachian hills. The house and the outbuildings were all painted white with green shingled roofs. Despite the fact that home for me meant being with my wife Sally and our two sons, I never lost my sense of that childhood home. When my family was young, each year, Sally and I and the boys would make the road trip back to Pennsylvania. As we got closer on the winding road, I would start to look for the green roof and the white house. I didn't want to miss my first glimpse of the farm. When we pulled in the drive, I always had a sense of being home.

That's an experience we all want. We love heading home. We love those familiar roads. We want to go where the lay of the land is burned in our memory, and where the people always made us feel as if we belonged.

When my parents were no longer able to keep the farm, they moved into more appropriate quarters. It fell to me as the oldest child to sell the farm. I found a buyer. We hosted an auction to sell the farm equipment and the various items our family had collected. What had been a place of nurture had become a place we could no longer maintain.

The following Christmas, Sally gave me a personalized calendar, with pictures of family and familiar places. With anticipation, I opened it to January. There was a photo of the family farm in western Pennsylvania with the white buildings and green roofs clearly visible. It caught me off guard. Tears filled my eyes. The place I called home now belonged to somebody else.

Jesus talked about the home of a well-to-do farmer with two grown sons. The younger son rebelled, left home, found new friends, and settled into a new home, but the new friends were fickle and his new home turned into a pigpen. What he wanted more than anything else was to go home.

In 1955, MGM made a movie called *The Prodigal*. It was Hollywood's remake of the story in Luke's Gospel told by Jesus. Ironically, the movie stars Lana Turner. It's ironic because there are no women in Jesus's story. Before the movie came out, Lana Turner at a press conference about the film said the movie was about juvenile delinquency. In the movie, the younger brother lived a wild life in Damascus. After going home, his father threw a big party. The younger son got the wealth; the other brother received nothing. The movie seems to say "Carousing pays off." The movie got two stars, but missed the point.

Carousing never pays off. Ask the families who have lost children to drunk drivers. Ask the men who can't remember who they slept with last night. Ask the wife who just cleaned up the kitchen again after her drunken husband came home. Ask the people with sexually transmitted diseases. Carousing never pays off.

We call it the story of the prodigal son, but the word "prodigal" doesn't appear in the biblical record. It's a word that means "lavish." The name stuck because it characterized the younger son's wasteful, extravagant living.

In the parable, the older son never left home. He tended to the farm. But Jesus revealed that all was not well with him either. He lived at the house but was never really at home. He ate with the father, but it seemed more like a one-night stand.

The story is often called the parable of the prodigal son, but it's not just about the younger son; it's also about the older son. But the more I read Luke 15, the more I see it's really about a father and two sons. In fact, it's about the father, not about the son who left but came back, nor about the son who never left but never felt at home. It's a story about a father.

Two lines in the story underline the twin themes of father and home. Luke 15:20 says, "But while he was yet at a distance, his father saw him." Later, when the older son pouts in the field, verse 28 tells us, "His father came out and entreated him." In both places, the father took the central role. He's waited for the younger son to come home, and he wanted his older son to embrace home. The point of both lines is "the father was ready."

Every Saturday morning, I pray for prodigals. I have a list of over one hundred fathers and mothers whose sons and daughters are far from home. They may live across the country or across the street, but they are not at home. Some days, I pray that the prodigals will come to their senses. Other days, I pray that the reason they left will become the reason they return. Mostly, I pray that the mother and father will be ready. I pray that while their son or daughter is at a great distance, the parent will see her or him and run and embrace them. I pray that the mother or father will go to the unhappy child and urge them to come home. I pray that they will be ready.

That's where we all find ourselves. Whether in our family or our church or our school, we know people who left. They wandered off. They ran away. They left in anger. The common thread is that we want them home.

In 1993, Jack Exum told a story in *Image Magazine* about a man with two sons. One day, the younger one asked his father for his share of the family estate. Shortly afterward, he left home, went far away, wasted the money, and made superficial friends. An economic recession left him without funds and hungry. He found work feeding pigs. In fact, he got so hungry he wanted to eat the pigs' food; but it was not to be.

Meanwhile, his older brother stayed home to work the farm. The two boys were close. They had formed a rich relationship through their childhood experiences. They shared common dreams. Both knew the older son should get to leave home first, but the younger brother thought traditions should be broken. So he left.

The older brother knew about the dangers of the big city. After his younger brother left, his father began to age prematurely. The older brother decided he had to act, so he told his father he would go search for his little brother. He packed his bags and promised to bring his brother home. He left the family farm with his father standing at the familiar spot where he stood each evening looking for his youngest son. This time, the father watched his oldest boy disappear over the horizon.

The older boy went from city to city, asking if anybody had seen his brother. He went door to door, business to business. He visited the unsavory parts of town. He called his brother's name as he walked down the streets. Then, he met some people who had known a wild young man of his brother's description, but they had lost track of him. Finally, the older brother came to a farmer and described his brother. The farmer said, "I know that boy. I hired him three months ago to feed my herd of swine. He's out in the field." As the older brother climbed the rocky hill outside of town, he saw a man dressed in rags, looking older than his years, with no shoes, covered with filth, his hair unwashed and matted. Thin and broken, he chewed on the husks of the corn the pigs were eating. The two embraced and wept. "I've come to take you home, brother."

They started home. The trip went quickly. One day, they came around the curve in the road and there was their father, tired and stooped over. When he saw them, he ran to meet them. He kissed them. He called for a celebration. They killed the fatted calf. The father told everybody in the neighborhood, "My sons were lost, but now they are found."[1]

We all know what Jack Exum has done. He's rewritten the story of the prodigal son. That's what God wants to do with all the prodigals. That's what he wants to do with my life. He wants to rewrite the lines. He wants all the prodigals to come home. He wants all the lost to be found.

God is ready. Are you?

Continuities. When we listen to the cries of the world's most vulnerable, one theme remains constant: they want a home. That means somebody has to make room.

WHAT DO YOU THINK?

1. Tell about the place you think of as home.

2. Tell about somebody you know who doesn't have a home.

---

[1] Jack Exum, "The Story of the Loving Brother," *Image*, July/August 1993, 22.

3. List ways in which we can help people find a home. Think in terms of the story in Luke 15.

4. Think about someone you know who is a prodigal. Is there some way you can minister to the prodigal's grandmother, grandfather, mother, father, or the prodigal herself?

20

SING FOR JOY

ISAIAH 49:13-16

Johnny Morrow, in his 1860 autobiography, *A Voice from the Newsboys*,[1] tells of his early happy childhood in Liverpool. Then his mother died, and his father remarried and took the family to New York City, where they lived in poverty. Their family of seven occupied a six-hundred-square-foot apartment where the oldest five children slept in one bed. Johnny recalled it was like being a sardine in a can. When Johnny turned ten, he became a street peddler. While working one day, he found a large piece of wood somebody had lost. When he picked it up, the owner saw him, accused him of stealing it, and beat Johnny until his legs bled. After telling his father what the man did, his own father gave him a second beating.

Later, he proposed that he could make money peddling matches on the street. His father approved and gave him a quarter. The next morning, Johnny bought ninety-seven books of matches, and by the end of day, had sold them all. As a reward, he bought himself two cakes and gave his father a dollar. Instead of buying food for the family, the father sent his daughter out for a bottle of brandy.

It's an old story with a familiar ring. Parents bring children into the world and then fail to help them grow up. A mother and father who should love the child end up acting in hateful ways.

---

[1] Cited in Stephen O'Connor, *Orphan Trains* (Boston: Houghton Mifflin, 2001), 116–47.

The Johnny Morrows keep coming. It's discouraging and makes us wonder how we can find perspective and how we can keep going. It makes us wonder where it all ends.

Katheryn Darr points out that much of the book of Isaiah revolves around two significant metaphors: children and women. We think of Isaiah 1:2: "Sons have I reared and brought up, but they have rebelled against me." More familiar is Isaiah 9:6: "For to us a child is born, to us a son is given." Isaiah later compares Jerusalem to a harlot and Zion to a mother. Isaiah gives children names that preach a sermon: Shearjashub, Immanuel, and Mahershalalhashbaz.

Darr points out that children of all ages appear in Isaiah: infants, youths, young adults. She refers six times to young children as examples of limited knowledge and competence, nine times to children to illustrate vulnerability, thirteen times to show the nature of love, and twenty times to speak about rebelliousness.[2]

Rather than take up all the children mentioned in Isaiah, consider the use of children in Isaiah 49. This chapter belongs to the larger section of Isaiah 40–55, and these chapters together contain some of the greatest words of assurance found in the Bible. Scholars call them salvation oracles. Isaiah offers assurance through incredible poetry eleven times in these sixteen chapters. One such oracle of salvation comes in Isaiah 49:13–16.

He wrote to Judeans who lived in Babylon in captivity. Many believed their God caused them to lose the last war. They doubted his existence and believed if he did exist, he didn't care about them. If he did care, they thought he must be powerless to do anything about their situation. They believed if he even knew about their situation, there was nothing he could do to make it better.

Then Isaiah imagined the earth being a chorus and the heavens a recording artist (Isa. 49:13). The song announced that God comforted his people and that they could expect compassion. Everything was all right.

The people, called Zion, spoke in verse 14. "The LORD has forsaken me; my Lord has forgotten me." Zion complained to God that he did not

[2] Katheryn Pfisterer Darr, *Isaiah's Vision and the Family of God*, (Louisville: Westminster John Knox, 1994), 13–84.

do what he said he would do. God's response used the image of children: "Can a woman forget her sucking child, that she should have no compassion on the son of her womb? Even these may forget, yet I will not forget you. Behold, I have graven you on the palms of my hands" (Isa. 49:15–16).

It's one of the few times that the Bible uses a feminine image to describe God. Could we find a woman who could forget the baby she's breastfeeding? Is there a mother who would not love the baby she carried in the womb?

Isaiah admitted that possibility. You might find a woman who has overlooked her child or one who treats her baby like garbage. It may be that those among us who care for at-risk children know those women.

But even if you could find a woman or two that would forget their child, God will never treat you that way. Never. They might forget, but God will not forget.

Isaiah wrote to the Judeans in Babylon. They believed God had forgotten them. God had destroyed their homes. He sent them into exile. They felt like he dumped them out in the middle of the night.

God will not forget, Isaiah says, because he has your name engraved on the palm of his hand. There tattooed on his hand are the names of people. Isaiah implied that he has my name engraved on his hand. Your name is there too.

I like to use the metaphor of an office. Suppose God had an office up in heaven. If you sat down in his big chair behind his large desk, you might look at the items carefully arranged on his desktop. Among the papers and other items, right there in the middle is your picture. He has you on his mind every day.

Like exiles, we often wonder if God cares. We join in the bitter music of our age, but God is off singing a new song. The Johnny Morrows keep coming. Fathers continue to desert their children. Mothers toss their babies out like garbage. We look out the window and think there's not much chance God will show up today. Despair, discouragement, and darkness invade our spirits.

When those discouraging times come, read Isaiah 49. He never forgets. Your name is engraved on his hand. Your picture is on his desk. Sing for joy.

Continuities. Life is complex. We hear more things than we can remember. So we listen and then we forget. We especially do that with the cries of the vulnerable. We hear. We are moved. We are touched. We forget. The mission of listening and making room belongs to God. He hears. He never forgets.

WHAT DO YOU THINK?

1. Why do you think Isaiah so frequently used children as illustrations?

2. Tell about a time you or a child you know was forgotten.

3. What difference does it make to know that God will not forget us?

4. Do you know any Johnny Morrows? As an individual, class, or a church, is anything being done for this child? If not, what can be done?

21

YOUR ROUTE GUIDANCE IS COMPLETE

GENESIS 1:27

Scott Dikkers and Oswald Pratt wrote a book in 1999 called *You Are Worthless.* It parodies the genre of inspirational self-help books. Chapter titles include "Your Good-for-Nothing Friends," "Your Miserable Job," and "Life: What's the Use?" At one point he writes, "You're no good, you're not great-looking, and you're going to die someday and it's probably going to hurt." He points out that the only reason your pet likes you is because you feed it. You don't have any outstanding qualities. In fact, you're pretty much like everybody else.[1]

A website entitled "Human for Sale" offers a set of extremely personal questions. It took me about five minutes to complete the questionnaire. At the end, it told me my value in dollars. In the comment section, others reported on their surveys. One man, disappointed with his net worth, concluded, "If anyone wants to take me for free, I will do anything you say just so you have to take me. I'm very poor."[2]

It's not hard to find hard evidence that humans have no value. The number of American babies killed by abortion each year is roughly equal

---

[1] Oswald T. Pratt and Scott Dikkers, *You Are Worthless: Depressing Nuggets of Wisdom Sure to Ruin Your Day* (Riverside, NJ: Andrews McMeel Publishing, 1999).
[2] www.humanforsale.com/, accessed October 1, 2018.

to all the Americans who died in all the wars of our nation.[3] One in nine people around the world go to bed hungry every night.[4] Marva Dawn, in her book *In the Beginning, God,* says it would take thirteen billion dollars to feed all those people and meet their health needs. That's less than what America spends each year on pet food.[5] The FBI reports over seventeen thousand people were murdered in the United States in 2016, and that was up over 8 percent from the year before. One in five American children live in poverty.[6]

Are humans worthless? Do we have no value? If we do have value, where does it come from?

Most of us use GPS. It tells us how to get where we are going. The greatest GPS program ever developed is the Bible. It tells us how to get where we want to go. It also tells us where we start. We start "in the beginning" (Gen. 1:1).

Genesis 1 unfolds like a pyramid. It moves through six creative days, with successive days treated in more detail than the one before. Events on day six take up the most space. The word "God" appears thirty-five times in Genesis 1. There are no eyewitnesses, no cameras, and no prophets in a viewing booth. We know what happened because God told us.

The chapter connects speech and act. God calls for light, and without pause or delay, there is light. God is in complete control. There are no other gods, no counterphilosophies, no presidents, no nations, no websites filled with objections. Nothing in the chapter tries to prove his existence. God just is. No one challenges his authority. He just is.

God in Genesis 1 might be compared to a conductor of an orchestra. He doesn't play all the instruments, but he controls all that happens. He is in charge. He's alive, well, strong, active, and great. He doesn't get tired, worn-out, sick, confused, depressed, or puzzled. He sees truly and acts

---

[3] "American Casualties: Abortions in the US Compared to World War II," Human Coalition, accessed December 19, 2018, https://www.humancoalition.org/graphics/american-casualties-abortions-us-compared-world-war-ii/.
[4] "Quick Facts: What You Need to Know About Global Hunger," Mercy Corps, accessed October 1, 2018, https://www.mercycorps.org/articles/quick-facts-what-you-need-know-about-global-hunger.
[5] Marva Dawn, *In the Beginning, God* (Downers Grove: InterVarsity Press, 2009), 54.
[6] Patrick T. McCarthy, *2017 Kids Count Data Book, State Trends in Child Well-Being* (Baltimore: Annie E. Casey Foundation, 2017), 13.

clearly. He doesn't wear sandals, use a cane, or have a long robe. He knows about lasers, nuclear physics, and digital communication.

Day six is most significant. On that day, God creates humanity. There, he lists five points on our GPS. It's where we start. Wherever you want to go, these five points indicate where we begin.

First, humans are made in his image. "So God created man in his own image, in the image of God he created him" (Gen. 1:27). The point appears twice (vv. 26–27). Anytime God repeats himself, we do well to listen. Of all the created items, we are the most like God. If we are like him, it says something about our value, worth, and importance.

Second, humans have dominion over the created world. Verse 26 says, "let them have dominion." That line also appears twice (vv. 26, 28). In effect, we are told to run the earth the way God would run it. It's the foundation of biblical ecology. Don't abuse the world, but make good use of it. We are to treat everything, including other people, the way God treated all he made. That means we have value as part of his creation.

Third, God blesses us and tells us to multiply. "And God blessed them, and God said to them, 'Be fruitful and multiply'" (v. 28). Blessing is the Bible's way of saying something is important or significant. God is in charge, and he says people are important to him. He told them to have children. Those children are important to him too. They have value.

Fourth, the humans and animals have plants for food (vv. 29–30). "Behold, I have given you every plant . . . ; you shall have them for food." In effect, God says he created enough food to go around. That line begins with the word "behold." That's the Bible's way of saying, "Pay attention!" This point is the beginning of a Bible-long crusade to make sure that the poor, the orphans, the widows, and the aliens get enough to eat. The underlying point is that God is a God of justice and fairness. He made enough to go around.

Fifth, God looks over all he created, including the humans, and his evaluation is that it's "very good" (v. 31). This point is introduced with another "behold." He's saying, "I didn't make any trash. Nothing here is disposable. It does not go out of style."

Ironically, Genesis 1 is the battlefield for the fight between the creationists and evolutionists. The reality is if Genesis 1 is not true, the implications are enormous. Human life has no value. We are just the result of random choices. Instead of blessing, only the strong survive. We lose the image, the blessing, and the command to take care of the world like God would. We lose track of the reality that there is enough food for all. We lose the "very good."

If we don't start here as Genesis 1 says, then we start in darkness. We begin in a world where might makes right. We start out without the fundamental truth of compassion or love or God. We're left to whoever has the most guns. We are left with the survival of the fittest.

But we start in Genesis 1. We are made to be like God. We run things the way he would run them. We have value and significance because he blessed us all. We call for justice for all people to have access to God's food.

We start in a very good world.

> **Continuities.** We listen and make room for the world's vulnerable because they have value and because even from the beginning, there was enough for them. God made room for them in the beginning. We do well to listen to what God said. The people of the Network 1:27 coalition chose Genesis 1:27 as one of their guiding passages. Like them, we must start at the right place if we hope to reach our destination.

WHAT DO YOU THINK?

1. When we take a trip, why is it important that we know our starting point?

2. Which of the five points in Genesis 1 strikes you as significant? Explain your answer.

3. If society believed all people were made like God and had value, what would change?

4. Cite something you have heard or read that points out humans have little value.

22

ALIVE TO GROWTH—
EVANGELISM
CLOSE TO HOME

1 CORINTHIANS 3:5-9

My friend Dan Cooper from New Jersey was teaching a lectureship class. About one hundred of us sat in the auditorium. He asked us to raise our hands if we had become Christians when we were children or teenagers. About ninety of us raised our hands. He said every time he asks that question, the ratio remains constant. His survey does not mean people do not become Christians later in life; it just means that most people who currently go to church started to follow Jesus as youths.

I understood Dan's statistic, but it took me years to see my own inconsistency. When I talked about evangelism, I meant we should win adults to Christ. As a result, we focused our mass mailings, our meetings, our outreach services on adults. When I thought of evangelism, I pictured a couple in their late twenties with a new baby now seeking God. We studied the Bible and they followed Jesus. I remembered the thirtysomething man who married one of the single women in our church. There was the sixty-year-old man who married one of our church widows. I presented the gospel to both men and baptized them into Christ. I spent a career in ministry focused on evangelizing adults. Yet, the statistics reveal most people come to Christ as children.

I did some calculating. The base numbers change from time to time, but the ratio stays steady. About one-third of all Americans are under twenty years of age. Let's be generous and say about half of them already go to church. That means of any total population, about one-sixth of the people who have no church home are children. If there are sixty thousand people within ten miles of a church building, about ten thousand of them (one-sixth of the total) are children who do not follow Jesus, who do not go to church, who have few sources of faith. Think of that number: ten thousand children who do not go to church.

I've attended elders' meetings for about fifty years. Elders seldom talk about children. Even less time is spent talking about children who do not go to church. I understand that children don't help make the budget. They don't put in the volunteer hours. They don't voice the complaints. But the numbers of children who do not have a source of faith are staggering!

Paul used two metaphors that explain this better. He said, "I planted, Apollos watered, but God gave the growth" (1 Cor. 3:6). His first metaphor compares evangelism to farming. Then he adds, "I laid a foundation, and another man is building upon it" (1 Cor. 3:10). This second metaphor compares sharing the gospel with construction. The foundation of the building is Jesus. We build. But if the foundation is Jesus, the structure stands.

The main point of both metaphors is that success doesn't come by human agency. God makes the seed grow and causes the building to stand. Compared to God, our task is easy. We plant and water. We dig and hammer. God makes it work.

When it comes to evangelism, most of us think of the hardest cases. How would I deal with the prodigal son if I met him in a far country? What would I say to the unrepentant thief on the cross? What if Festus's or Agrippa's salvation depended on my presentation of the gospel? How can I convince that atheist at work? What do I study with the man who attempted suicide? Do I try to convert our neighbor who swears at our dog?

But most evangelism is not hard. Most planting is done with children and teens. The gospel begins with telling a child a Bible story for the first time. It means being the first adult to really listen to a teenager. It means being a friend to a college student away from home. None of that is hard.

Evangelism starts close to home. If you work in the nursery teaching children the concept of God, you are a seed planter. Teach the two-year-old "Jesus Loves Me"? You are a builder. Give a blessing to a first grader? You are a waterer. Invite the neighbor's children to Vacation Bible School? You are a carpenter. Put on a puppet show for children? You are a farmer. Teach the plan of salvation to the fifth graders? You build for God. Lead a small group at Christian camp? Talk to a teenager one-on-one about Jesus? Pick up a child from an unchurched home and bring him to services? You harvest for God.

I don't understand why we don't have long lines of people waiting to teach children in Bible class. Children and teenagers are unplanted, unwatered fields. They have no sophisticated arguments against the gospel. They have no ill-conceived theology to correct. They are souls waiting for seed, hearts waiting for water.

If we do not plant and do not water, the results are serious. If we don't build, the movie industry will. If we don't harvest, the secular songwriters will. If we don't plant, their friends will.

Society plants weeds. They tell little girls that unless they look like a cover girl, they are nothing. They communicate to little boys that unless you can dunk the ball, you are nothing. Young people are fed a diet of sex without responsibility, instant gratification without effort, solutions without sacrifice, that life is about getting rather than giving, and that self must be preserved over community.

Years ago, I heard about a Christian man on the West Coast. He reported talking to a teenage girl he knew from church. She asked him, "Do you know why I spent so much of my junior and senior high years at your house?" He replied that he thought she was good friends with his daughter. The teen said, "Yes, but there was another reason. When I came into your house, I got a hug when I came in and when I left. I never got them at home."

One out of six Americans may be in that young woman's situation, waiting, hoping, needing love and affection. That man planted seeds and watered a young plant.

I grew up in an unchurched home. Neither my parents nor my grandparents went to church. As a child, I was an empty field. Mildred Stutzman, the wife of a potato farmer, came along and planted a seed. As a neighborhood child, I attended her Vacation Bible School class. After it was over, she followed up and invited me to Sunday school. Ray Beggs, the new preacher, came along and watered. He started a Wednesday night teenage class and came to my house and invited me to come. I learned about God from Mildred and about the gospel from Ray. One Wednesday night during that class, I decided to follow Jesus.

Ninety percent of us became Christians as children. Kingdom growth starts small. What are you doing?

Continuities. Listening and making room for the vulnerable of the world encompasses a range of activities that God includes in the mission. It includes listening to the unwanted child thrust into foster care, but also teaching that room full of four-year-olds on Sunday morning. Don't make this harder than it is. Listening and making room can easily occur on Sunday morning at 9:30.

WHAT DO YOU THINK?

1. Who first taught you about God? When did you learn *Jesus Loves Me*?

2. Make a list of ten children you know who do not go to church. Discuss what you might do to plant and water their lives.

3. Are children of outsiders welcome in your congregation? Give evidence.

4. How can we use our homes to become planters and waterers of the gospel?

23

GETTING THE HEARTS OF OUR CHILDREN IN THE RIGHT PLACE

DEUTERONOMY 6:4-9

Several years ago, Sally and I worshipped with a rural congregation in southeastern Ohio. The old white clapboard building sat atop a hill. On the west side was a large cemetery. The date on the cornerstone was 1880.

Before services, I talked to Charlotte, a middle-aged woman, who reminisced about her childhood when the church building was filled every Sunday. About eight people attend now. I asked her what happened. She said most of the people either died or were doing drugs.

It reminds us all of the sad stories of people whose children are prodigals. They are among the "nones"—the rapidly growing number of people who do not go to any church or have any faith.

Something's missing. The children are not getting the core message. It's not enough to be in church or to be in Sunday school. Something more has to happen. It takes me back to Deuteronomy.

This fifth book of the Old Testament centers on the next generation. Most of the older Israelites died in the wilderness. Moses spent his last moments trying to pass the faith on to the next generation. He told them how to keep faith in a hostile culture. Throughout the book, Moses returned to the future of children.

Jesus had strong feelings about Deuteronomy. When he fasted in the wilderness for forty days and then faced the tempter, he responded to Satan all three times by quoting Deuteronomy. When he was asked about the greatest commandment, he went to Deuteronomy. Jesus pointed to Deuteronomy 6:4–9 as a central biblical teaching:

> Hear, O Israel: The LORD our God is one LORD; and you shall love the LORD your God with all your heart, and with all your soul, and with all your might. And these words which I command you this day shall be upon your heart; and you shall teach them diligently to your children, and shall talk of them when you sit in your house, and when you walk by the way, and when you lie down, and when you rise. And you shall bind them as a sign upon your hand, and they shall be as frontlets between your eyes. And you shall write them on the doorposts of your house and on your gates.

Moses said, "Love the LORD." Love in Deuteronomy is a commanded love, not an emotion. Moses used a variety of terms to convey the meaning of loving God: serve him, fear him, cling to him, walk with him, keep his commandments. In short, it means loyalty.

In this passage, Moses called God's followers to love him with our heart, soul, and might. *Heart* refers to the intellect or the mind. *Soul* points to life or to our humanity. *Might* means our power and resources. The Old Testament often lists concepts like this one in a merism: a figure of speech that uses different terms to denote the parts of one larger thing. We talk about hook, line, and sinker. It means everything. We search every nook and cranny. It means we've looked everywhere. Heart, soul, and might means with all you have, with all you are, with all of your life. It means put your whole being, your whole energy, your whole existence into loving God.

This core command goes in two directions. First, put it on your heart. Keep it in the core of your being. Second, teach this command diligently to your children. The word "diligently" is a word associated with something "sharp." Deuteronomy 32:41 uses it as "whet" in the phrase "if I *whet* my glittering sword." Just as God sharpens his sword of justice, so we sharpen the hearts of our children's love for God. In Psalm 73:21, the writer talks about his embittered heart and uses the word "pricked." It says, "I was *pricked* in heart." Just as the enemy's sword made the writer's heart bitter, we must pierce the heart of our children with the love of God.

We teach our children to love God with their heart, soul, and might; that is, with all they have. They are to think about loving God when they sit, lie down, and rise up; that is, in everything they do. They are to have his love on their hands and foreheads; that is, all that they are. They are to write it on the doorposts and gates; that is, everywhere they go.

We must teach children to love God. It is not so much how we teach, but what we teach. It is not where we teach them, but what we teach them. It is not when we teach them, but what we teach them.

Here is the core issue: *If God gets the heart of our children, then he gets our children.* It's not legalism that says you must write the love of God on your doorpost, but not in your kitchen. Our homes, our lives, our churches must declare that we love God. If the love of God gets in the hearts of our children, then God gets them for life.

When we left that rural church in southeastern Ohio that Sunday, I noticed that they had an old wrought iron sign in front of the building. The letters were formed out of bent iron. It originally said "Church of Christ," but the first "h" in church was missing. It said "C_urch of Christ."

I've thought a great deal about how that one congregation mirrors our whole age. It almost seemed to me that the missing "h" stood for "heart." When we and our children don't have the love of God in our hearts, the results are disastrous. When God gets our hearts, God gets us. The first few verses of Deuteronomy 6 remind us:

> Hear, O Israel: The LORD our God is one LORD; and you shall love the LORD your God with all your heart, and with all your soul, and with all your might. And these words which I command you this day shall be upon your heart; and you shall teach them diligently to your children . . .

Continuities. Listening and making room can be done in a variety of ways. Teaching is a powerful means of influencing the world's vulnerable and of carrying out God's mission. Are you listening for those who have not been taught? Do you make room in your class for those who have never heard?

WHAT DO YOU THINK?

1. List the specific ways your congregation teaches children to love God. Describe the moment when this teaching takes place. Avoid general answers such as "we have Sunday school." Instead, tell when and where in Sunday school children are instructed to love God.

2. Do you agree with the statement, "If God gets the heart of our children, then he gets our children"? Explain your answer.

3. What are some of the reasons our children are not getting the core message to love God with all their heart? What can we do differently as parents and teachers?

24

NOW IS THE TIME
TO SPEAK UP

PROVERBS 31:8-9

In the summer of 1974, Sally and I participated in the archaeological excavations at Tel Aphek/Antipatris. It is located a few miles from Tel Aviv, Israel. The place was the site of the Israelite–Philistine battle in 1 Samuel 4. Later in Acts 23, after Paul was arrested in Jerusalem, he was taken by armed guard to Caesarea. They overnighted in Antipatris. Today, the site contains a large mound that includes a Crusader fortress and a World War I British army barracks.

When we arrived midseason, most of the excavation team was gathered around the Ping-Pong table observing and arguing about a piece of pottery about the size of the book you are reading. They discovered the piece of pottery in excavations at a nearby site called Izbet Sartah, which many identify with biblical Ebenezer of 1 Samuel 4:1. The archaeologists dug down about six inches and uncovered remains from the Late Bronze period, about the time of the judges. This large piece of pottery had lines on it. The argument at the Ping-Pong table raged over whether the lines were made by roots growing next to the shard over the centuries or whether the lines represented writing. They asked one of the Americans who knew no ancient languages to write down what he saw. He looked at the potsherd and started to draw. The archaeological experts were amazed. He was writing an ancient script of biblical Hebrew!

We now know it is one of the oldest examples of Hebrew writing in the world. The potsherd, now called an ostracon because of the writing, contains seventy-seven letters. They make up several listings of the Hebrew alphabet. The archaeologists speculate that a Late Bronze Age child learning to write practiced his or her alphabet on that broken piece of pottery.

We have the homework of a child that lived three thousand years ago! I suspect we all hope that archaeologists do not dig up our homework centuries from now.

It made me wonder, when did education for children begin? Isaiah 2 speaks about a school in Jerusalem where people came to study. A French archaeologist, André Lemaire, argued that ancient Israel did have schools and that some of the books of the Old Testament were their texts. He suggested that Proverbs may have been one of the key texts in these schools.[1] From Proverbs, the children learned about morality, discipline, priorities, values, and the best way to live life. They would also have learned about children.

If Proverbs served as a schoolbook for young Israelite children, then the final chapter takes on significant meaning. Young girls see a vision for their life in the poem about the virtuous woman in Proverbs 31:10–31. Young boys might have seen their vision for life in Job 31:1–40, which describes the virtuous man. Not all children would have good parents who saw to their education, so part of the child's education involved an obligation to other children. So near the end of the book of Proverbs we have these lines in 31:8–9:

Open your mouth for the dumb,
    for the rights of all who are left desolate.
Open your mouth, judge righteously,
    maintain the rights of the poor and needy.

Some people are physically or socially mute. They cannot speak or will not speak. In the line "rights of all who are left desolate," the word "rights" comes from the same Hebrew word as the name Daniel, which means

---

[1] André Lemaire, *Les écoles et la formation de la Bible dans l'ancien Israel* (Gottingen: Vandenshoeck und Ruprecht, 1981), 39.

"God is my judge." The verse tells us that somebody with a voice should seek the rights of those who do not have a voice. It means to advocate for the unfortunate. The word behind "desolate" means the unfortunate or the ones vanishing away. Literally, it reads the "sons of those dying." It would be hard to find a better description of unwanted, orphaned, and foster children than to see them as the ones for whom all protectors and nurturers are vanishing away. If verse 8 speaks about the people involved, then verse 9 spells out the action. "Judge righteously" might be translated "work so that these unfortunate enjoy the kind of life you do." It's a pocket version of the Golden Rule (Matt. 7:12). All people have a right to life, safety, education, housing, work, and family. We should speak for those missing one or more of those items.

Let me suggest three ways in which we, the children of God, learn the same lessons that the children in Ebenezer and elsewhere learned from their ancient schoolbooks. We can use these in being the kind of people envisioned at the end of Proverbs.

First, speak on behalf of children. Don and Denise are good friends of ours. They heard about a child that the Memphis police found in a pile of trash on an inner-city street. They had no connection with this child, but they quickly saw that this little girl had no voice. So they began to advocate for her. Eventually, they adopted this little girl into their own family. I saw her not long ago. She's now a young adult with a smile on her face. Somebody spoke up for her.

A few years ago, I wrote a book called *Children Mean the World to God*. One of the points of the book is that in most congregations, children are in third or fourth place behind the church leaders and the other adults. Since they don't serve as leaders or put much money in the plate, their concerns get pushed aside. Adults make decisions for the church. Sometimes the children have no voice at all. Whether it is a child in a pile of garbage or the children in the nursery at your congregation, speak up for children.

Second, speak for the vulnerable. While living in Memphis, my friend Buster Clemens saw that many elderly and disabled people in the city could not properly maintain the homes they owned and lived in. He harnessed the energy of teenagers and every summer gathered over four hundred energetic teens to paint more than thirty houses. Painting was his way of speaking up for the vulnerable.

Another friend, Jeff Dimick, lived in Los Angeles. When Hurricane Katrina struck southern Louisiana, he formed Hilltop Mission, gathered a group of workers to travel 2,000 miles, and spent a combined 26,000 hours mucking over 1,650 homes. That initial cleanup was his way of speaking up for the vulnerable.

Third, speak on behalf of God. A few years ago, I was called to the bedside of a well-known church hater and atheist. Dying of AIDS, he asked his mother to send for a preacher. I got the call. When I arrived, I did not know what to say. So I spoke on behalf of God. I held his hand and prayed Psalm 23. I spoke the words of God to that young man. When I finished, he smiled and drifted into unconsciousness. A few days later, he died.

Speak on behalf of children. Say a word for the sake of the vulnerable. On appropriate occasions, say the words of God to those who desperately need to hear his voice.

Today you can go to a museum in Jerusalem and see the Aphek ostracon—penned by an unknown student, likely a child, or perhaps somebody older, just doing their homework. But those squiggly lines are a voice from the past reminding us that education is important and that at the core of what God teaches us to do is to speak for those who have no voice.

Continuities. God provides nearly all of us with ears to hear. He gives us voices to speak. He generously offers us the use of his home. Some do not have ears, a voice, or a home. Listening and making room often means speaking out for those who cannot speak or who are never heard.

WHAT DO YOU THINK?

1. Describe your earliest memory of being a student.
2. Tell of a time you taught a child something.

3. Why is teaching so powerful?

4. List opportunities that your congregation might use for teaching those who remain untaught.

5. What child do you need to speak up for in your family, church, or neighborhood?

25

WAIT FOR ME

ISAIAH 49:20-23

Katheryn Darr, in a book entitled *Isaiah's Vision and the Family of God,* calls attention to how the prophet Isaiah used children as metaphors of the problems of the ancient world.[1] For example, Isaiah chose children to describe the horrors of war. He tells of infants "dashed in pieces before their eyes" (Isa. 13:15–16). His point is that the state of children often reflects the condition of society as a whole.

Our age tends to center more on numbers and less on such metaphors. According to *2018 Kids Count Data Book,* the 2010 U.S. Census failed to count nearly one million U.S. children under the age of five.[2] Stephen O'Connor's story of Charles Loring Brace's efforts to help U.S. orphans from 1854 to 1929 gives an update on children in his book *Orphan Trains.* When he wrote the book in 2001, some thirty-two thousand children were in foster care in New York City. Every change in federal or local politics affected the budget for these children and the services they received. Social workers sign on to help these children, yet he reported that every year, one out of every three social workers quits. New York City paid social workers less than sanitation workers.[3] Mayors and presidents come and go, budgets change, and social workers turn over. In the meantime, children die, foster

---

[1] Darr, *Isaiah's Vision and the Family of God*, 13–84.
[2] Patrick T. McCarthy, *2018 Kids Count Data Book* (New York: Annie E. Casey Foundation, 2018), 4.
[3] Stephen O'Connor, *Orphan Trains* (New York: Houghton Mifflin, 2001), 320–29.

care remains a national problem, those serving children call for help, and America and its churches go about their business. In a metaphorical sense, children are dashed to pieces before our eyes.

All these situations recall another passage from Isaiah 49. Children had died. They faced an unsolved national problem. Some seeking to find solutions to the problem called for help, while others just quit. Even the people of faith turned a deaf ear.

Isaiah's passage on children comes in the sixteen chapters of Isaiah 40–55, which take up three themes. Writing to people who were homeless and far from home, first he offered delightful words of reassurance. Second, he made some of the most extensive arguments for the existence of God anywhere in the Bible. Third, he told them to deal with the unsettled conditions in their world by being servants.

Isaiah described a future time when the mothers would have so many children that the young ones would complain about how crowded they were and ask the parents to add a room to the house. In response, God would call the nations around Israel to offer assistance. Rescue workers from those nations would come to take care of the children. A king would take in an Israelite youngster as a foster child and a queen would serve as a surrogate nursing mother. God concludes by saying, "I will save your children" (Isa. 49:20–23, 25). In verse 14, Zion complained to God because he had sent them into exile and had forsaken and forgotten them. In response, God spent the rest of the chapter giving evidence that he comforted and cared for Israel.

He compared their plight to a barren woman who had no children and had lost everything. She seemed to be alone, vulnerable, and helpless. But God responded that it is not true. She was not alone but had so many children that she would have to add on to the house.

In the second family metaphor, God compared their situation to that of orphans. Those homeless people were like orphans who had no parents. No one took care of them. They were like thousands of foster children in the United States who overwhelm the system, causing social workers to quit.

But God came to the rescue. They were adopted by kings and queens. They found themselves in a new home where the father was the monarch and money was of no concern. The newborns were breastfed by the queen mother.

On the east side of Nashville is the Hermitage, the home purchased in 1804 by Andrew Jackson, the seventh U.S. president. He and his wife Rachel had no biological children, so they adopted Andrew Jr. and Lyncoya. Then they watched over eight others, six boys and two girls from three different families. Imagine losing your parents and then being taken in by the president of the country. Everybody else calls him "Mr. President," but you call him "Dad." They call her the "First Lady," but you simply refer to her as "Mom."

The Hebrew word for "foster father" comes from the same root as the word "nurse." Mordecai became Esther's foster father just as a patient has a nurse. Naomi took little Obed from Ruth and became his nurse. The same root becomes the word faith.

Isaiah shows how the same root applied to God. He is faithful to us. He becomes our nurse. The two words "faithful" and "nurse" have a direct connection with perhaps the most widely known Hebrew word in the world: "Amen." It means "I am for you." God took these homeless people and made the king their foster father. It was God's way of saying, "I'm for you!"

This passage addresses one of our deepest issues. Those homeless people in Isaiah 40–55 wanted to give up. They didn't think God was up to the task of taking care of them. They thought their problems were bigger than God's capacity. We fall into the same way of thinking.

Stephen O'Connor, in *Orphan Trains*, tells of talking to a child in foster care in New York City. He asked, "What is life like from the point of view of a child in the American foster care system?" Here's what he said,

> One time I went through five, six workers in a three-month period. They'd just decide they wanted to leave, and I'd end up getting a new social worker, a new social worker, a new social worker. They'd leave because a lot of them told me they're overworked, underpaid, and on high stress. A lot of them told me you have to do this kind of work because you love it. You can't do it for the money. They left, and they were so happy—some went back to school, some went to other agencies. A couple I

stayed in contact with, and they said, "I'm so relaxed! My blood pressure is down!" They got their youth back.[4]

House parents give up. Directors of child care agencies get exhausted. Adoptive parents throw up their hands. Foster parents say, "No more." Social workers quit.

Like the homeless people in Isaiah, we feel overwhelmed. We think our problems are too big for God to handle. Isaiah helps us in three ways:

First, Isaiah corrects our thinking. If we believe God can't handle this problem, that thinking reflects a worldly way of reasoning. When we begin thinking in unbiblical ways, we come to unbiblical ends. When we reason in biblical ways, God responds.

Second, Isaiah tells us what to do. In Isaiah 49:23, God tells us, "Wait for me." Isaiah instructed the discouraged to wait for God. History revealed that God did all he said he would do. God is worth waiting for. The problem is not that God is not helping, but that we are not waiting.

Third, Isaiah reported on what God will do. In 49:25, he said, "I will save your children." The audience in Isaiah 40–55 thought God was powerless. God responded with one of the biggest promises of all time. "I will save your children."

Isaiah did not address our situation. He was not referring to losing house parents or social workers or government regulations. He was not talking about elderships that stop supporting child care or children with attachment disorders. He was not speaking about the situation we face.

But Isaiah did speak about the same God we serve. Listen to what he said: "I will save your children."

That's something worth listening to. God is big enough. God will save the children. Wait and you will not be put to shame.

Continuities. Did the prophecies of Isaiah ever come true? The negative answer comes in the last four chapters of the book. In short, the people did not wait on God. In our efforts to listen and make room, we must wait on God.

---

[4] O'Connor, *Orphan Trains*, 320.

WHAT DO YOU THINK?

1. Hundreds of thousands of American children are in foster care. What do you think about that number? Why are so many children in foster care?

2. When the exiles were discouraged, God used the metaphor of having children to give them hope. What do you think of that illustration?

3. God said his unwanted people would be like orphans adopted by kings and queens. Why did Isaiah make such a claim?

4. If you believed that God would save the unwanted American children, what difference would that make in your life and the work of your church?

5. Which of the three points that the author makes from Isaiah do you most need to hear and follow? Why?

26

WHEN A CHILD ASKS

DEUTERONOMY 6:20-25

C. S. Lewis tells of watching a group of children at the beach. They were not out in the water enjoying the surf, or on the shore building sandcastles, or walking along the beach picking up seashells; they were focusing on broken pieces of glass. Somebody had left their trash, and the children were playing with the shattered bottles.

Lewis makes the point that children are so easily influenced that if they are not properly guided, they go to the beach and play with broken shards of glass. Then he added, "The world is filled with trash."[1]

We regularly expose young children to violence, sex, consumerism, and addictive substances. Guns and gangs, pornography and sexually explicit language in movies, greed and avarice are readily consumed by many children growing up in the United States. The world is filled with trash.

Contrast our skill in raising children with our cultural abilities in other areas. We excel in creating apps for our phones that seem to do almost anything. We can put hundreds of wind turbines on every mountain ridge or windswept plain to generate electricity and add it to the grid. We can manufacture a car that will start itself, drive into the parking lot, and stop between the two yellow lines, all without a human driver. We can do all that and more, but seem unable to raise up a generation that avoids the trash. Too many children grow into adults that engage in violence and crime, vice

---

[1] Cited by Marshall Shelley, "The Sightless, Wordless, Helpless Theologian," *Christianity Today*, April 26, 1993.

and promiscuity, drugs and alcohol, and in far too many cases live lives of quiet desperation. The world is full of trash.

The situation raises serious questions. How can we live in one of the world's more advanced nations and yet raise generation after generation of young people to focus on the world's trash? Does this situation have anything to do with you and me? Does it have anything to do with the church? What does God think? What does the Bible have to say?

The longest passage in the Bible about passing on morals and faith to the next generation comes in Deuteronomy 6. Moses probably preached the three sermons of Deuteronomy on one day—the day he died. His audience was made up of the younger generation. Most of the older generation had died in the wilderness. The young people of Israel stood before him. One of the chief concerns of Deuteronomy is whether the next generation will follow God. When they enter the Promised Land, will they focus on the treasures of God or the trash of Canaan? One way of viewing this chapter is to see it as five principles for passing the faith on to the next generation. They are not hard to understand or new for the most part. We can summarize them briefly.

First, in order to pass on the faith to the next generation, young people must see the faith being lived. Deuteronomy 6:1–3 takes up this issue. Moses told them to do what God said, but he spent most of these three verses talking about the benefits of following God. You will live longer, get the land, and have children. Verse 2 is critical. When your children and their children see you obeying God, they will learn to do the same. Young people must have models.

Second, according to Deuteronomy 6:4–9, children must be taught. Jesus quoted these verses in Matthew 22 and said it was the great commandment. These lines come up again in Luke 10, where Jesus calls them the way to eternal life. Read them carefully. In the middle of this passage about loving God, Moses told the Israelites, "You shall teach them diligently to your children" (Deut. 6:7). When Judaism formed in exile, they began to recite these verses twice a day. Children must be taught to love God.

Third, young people must be warned that affluence breeds spiritual amnesia. Deuteronomy 6:10–15 notes that when they moved into the land

and lived in cities they did not construct and houses they did not build, and when they ate from trees and vines they did not plant, and drank water from cisterns that they did not dig, they would forget the LORD. When we have things, we tend to focus on the gift, not on the giver. Affluence can damage faith. Young people must be prepared for that negative challenge.

Fourth, Deuteronomy 6:16–19 provides another warning. Young people need to know that the problems of life will challenge their faith. Moses cited the events at Massah when they had no water. Humans can't survive long without water. They forgot they needed God as much as they needed water. The tragedies and pains and losses of life challenge faith. Young people must be prepared to face those issues.

Fifth, young people must be taught that faith rests on grace. In Deuteronomy 6:20–25, Moses told of a child with a question. The child wanted to know, Why do we have all these laws? Moses answered with a story. Basically, it has three points. We were slaves, and God set us free. He did it by grace. We were homeless in the wilderness, and God gave us land. He did it by his grace. We were clueless about how to live the good life. God gave us his book. He did it by grace. Young people must understand the foundational principle of grace.

That's a quick summary of the thesis of Deuteronomy. Young people need to have models, must be taught, must be warned about affluence and the problems of life, and they must understand grace.

What does this mean to you? What does it mean to the church you attend? What does it mean to our nation? Let me make two concluding observations.

First, these principles give us hope. Often, the trash of our world gets us down. I hear people in church praying regularly that God would fix our country and our government. Those are often prayers of despair, not hope.

Right now, wherever you are and wherever you go to church, there is a young boy within a couple of blocks. There are hundreds more within a few miles. This boy doesn't go to church. He is not being taught about God. He doesn't hate God. He's not an atheist.

He could grow up to be another C. S. Lewis. Or he could grow up to be another drug addict or incarcerated felon. But there is one absolutely certain truth about that little boy: somebody is going to teach him. He'll be taught the ways of the world or he'll be taught the ways of God.

Not far away from where you are reading this book is a precious little girl. She has no connection with any people of faith. She's just pure and innocent. She could become the next mayor of your city or the next Sunday school teacher in your church, or she could become the next streetwalker in your city, or the next person who gets drunk and runs a red light and kills a friend of yours. Somebody will teach that little girl. She might be taught the ways of the world. Or she might be instructed by a godly soccer coach or a good Sunday school teacher or by somebody like you. But she will be taught.

The great hope of these principles is that the next generation can come to faith if they hear about God. God depends on us to do that.

Second, it takes all of the older generation to raise up the next generation. I often hear people in our churches say that "I've retired from teaching children's Sunday school." I know of congregations where church leaders cancel VBS because nobody will teach the children. Too many Christians say, "I did my part when I was younger" or "I'm too busy." I'm sorry, but that attitude is totally unbiblical. You never retire. You never get to quit. You are supposed to attend to priorities. You are supposed to teach children until you no longer have the capacity to do so. Deuteronomy 6 calls all of the older generation to rise up and teach and mentor and pass on the faith to the next generation.

Let me be perfectly clear. Read this carefully. Jesus called it the Great Commandment:

> Hear, O Israel: The LORD our God is one LORD; and you shall love the LORD your God with all your heart, and with all your soul, and with all your might. And these words which I command you this day shall be upon your heart; and you shall teach them diligently to your children.

You shall teach them diligently to your children. When a child asks, teach them.

Continuities. The world teems with vulnerable, untaught children. Some of them are in the foster care system. Others are in your congregation. Listening and making room starts at home, now, with you.

WHAT DO YOU THINK?

1. Pick one of the five points made by Moses. When did you learn that lesson?

2. Which of the five points made by Moses seem to be most lacking in our homes and churches? Explain.

3. Name the different ways in which Christians can teach. Which ones are offered by your congregation? Which ones do you participate in?

4. How did you respond to the line, "'I've retired from teaching children's Sunday school.' I'm sorry, but that attitude is totally unbiblical"?

5. List some reasons you believe we are failing to pass on the faith to our children.

PART 4

MAKING ROOM

Making room means making changes. Making those changes comes through discipleship. If we deny ourselves and take up his cross and follow him, we will find a way to make the changes necessary to make room.

27

WOULD YOU BE POURED OUT LIKE WINE?

PHILIPPIANS 2:17

The *State of America's Children Yearbook* included a piece by Cliff Johnson, who told of a young mother bringing her child into the waiting room of the Nutrition Program for Women, Infants, and Children.[1] One of the weary caseworkers saw the baby drinking from a bottle filled with red liquid. The worker began to scold the mother: "You know babies don't need sugar drinks."

The mother started to respond but broke into tears. She finally revealed that she had spent all her money the previous week. She used her last funds to buy baby formula. It ran out the day before. The mother had not eaten in three days. "I didn't know what to do."

She went to a fast food restaurant with no money. She filled the baby's bottle with water and ketchup, two things that are free. The baby was not drinking a sugar drink but watered-down ketchup.

The story ended there. We wonder, "Did that woman get help? Was she using drugs? Did the child survive? Are they still in poverty?"

We love the stories where the evidence shows we made a difference, where the mother gets a job, where the baby grows up and goes to college. But we know many of the stories don't end that way. Instead, there are more drugs, more watered-down ketchup, more poverty, and more vulnerability.

---

[1] The story appears in the *State of America's Children Yearbook 1996,* page xiii, published by the Children's Defense Fund.

That's what happened to the apostle Paul. He established a congregation in the Macedonian city of Philippi. Later, he heard disturbing news.
Instead of cooperation, some in the congregation chose envy and rivalry
(Phil. 1:15). Instead of a common mission, they majored in partisanship
and insincerity (Phil. 1:17). Rather than sharing the truth, some peddled
pretense (Phil. 1:18). Casting aside unity, it was "us versus them" (Phil. 1:28).
Some grumbled. Others questioned (Phil. 2:14). Conditions disintegrated
to the point that Paul called some of them "dogs . . . evil-workers . . . those
who mutilate the flesh" (Phil. 3:2). A few lived as "enemies of the cross of
Christ" (Phil. 3:18). He even named names, calling on Syntyche and Euodia
to move beyond what troubled them (Phil. 4:2).

Paul had shared the gospel of love while he was with them. Now they
had gone another direction. Instead of focusing on others, they centered
on themselves. Instead of pulling each other up, they pushed each other
down. Instead of working side by side, they fussed from one point to
another. Paul preached in Philippi and now wrote from a jail cell in Rome.
It filled Paul with sorrow and anxiety (Phil. 2:27–28).

Most of us know that story. We've worked hard, but with little results.
We hoped for the best and got the worst. The people we tried to serve
rejected our help. They made promises and then broke them. They made
progress and then went backward. They made provisions and then
lost them.

Paul did three things in response. *First, he called them to do better.*
Don't grumble. Don't complain. Hold fast to what you agreed to do. He
didn't want to grow old thinking he'd won the race when he had lost it
(Phil. 2:16).

Second, he saw the good above the bad. In some ways, the four chapters
of Philippians work like a thank-you card. Paul told them that they made
a difference for him. He referred to the good times they had (Phil. 1:3). He
recalled their partnership in the gospel (Phil. 1:5; 4:3). They supported him
even after he went to prison (Phil. 1:7). He felt their love (Phil. 1:9), sensed
their prayer support (Phil. 1:19), applauded their progress in the faith (Phil.
3:15), and acknowledged that they shared his troubles (Phil. 4:14). He sent
Epaphroditus to help them (Phil. 2:25). Twice, they had sent him money
(Phil. 4:16).

Wouldn't you like to be the Philippians? Help Paul and then get mentioned in the New Testament! Surely the positive influence they had on Paul would get them nice condos on Pearl Street in heaven. It's nice to make a difference.

But we don't always make a difference. What happens when we do good and get taken to jail? How do we respond when the people we sought to help instead reject us, respond in a spiteful way, and fight? That leads to Paul's *third* response: a call to discipleship.

Paul makes this remarkable statement: "Even if I am to be poured as a libation upon the sacrificial offering of your faith, I am glad and rejoice with you all" (Phil. 2:17). Poured out. It takes us back to the Passover regulations in Leviticus 23:13. The priest took a quart of wine to the altar. He poured it out as a gift to God. The wine ran over the wood, down the rocks, onto the ground. None of the wine touched human lips. It satisfied no thirst. It entered no stomach. It was all poured out.

It takes us back to Jesus: "For the Son of man also came not to be served but to serve, and to give his life as a ransom for many" (Mark 10:45). Discipleship. Poured out like wine.

It takes us back to John's statement: "By this we know love, that he laid down his life for us; and we ought to lay down our lives for the brethren" (1 John 3:16). Discipleship. Poured out like wine.

It takes us back to Paul's model in Philippians 2. He calls us to have the mind of Christ. Jesus took the form of a servant. He humbled himself. He obediently went to the cross (Phil. 2:5–8). "Give his life." "Lay down his life." "Emptied himself." "Poured out like wine."

Philippians points to the costs of serving others. Service can lead to prison, hunger, abuse, disappointment, or fussing. Following Jesus might make us heroes; but more likely, doormats. It can lead to celebration or suffering. We can make the news or live in obscurity. It raises the question: Are we willing to be poured out like wine if we don't amount to more than a drop in a bucket?

We expect to be poured out like wine and then check the stats, see if the data looks good, count the baptisms, and see how we affected the poverty rate. Making a difference makes being poured out like wine worthwhile.

But Philippians, the thank-you letter about making a difference, also calls us to be poured out like wine when we don't make a difference and when we get no thanks. It happens all the time.

Wayne, a friend of mine, worked at a social service ministry at St. Anne's Church in New York City. He made friends with John Cossack, a homeless man. Local shopkeepers said nobody feared John, who preferred gentleness over violence. He lived in the doorways of Brooklyn Heights for twenty years. The son of a physician, John depended on the area shops for food. At noon every day, he'd stand on Henry Street leaning on a cane, asking for change. The park supervisor said he washed in the park restroom every day.

One August day, Wayne arrived at work to find a crowd gathered around the door of St. Anne's Church and police lights blinking along the street. The body of John Cossack slumped against the door, his throat slit, and his blood on the door. He was sixty-three. The police said he was killed for a bottle of wine.

My friend tried to help John. The crassest among us might say, "A lot of good he did. All he got to show for his effort was blood stains on the door."

Paul wants to know, "Are you willing to be poured out like wine for people like that?"

Will you give your all for people who don't give back at all? Are you willing to be poured out into a bucket that leaks? What if all you pour out amounts to just a drop in the bucket? Will you be poured out when your service is so utterly insignificant that nobody will remember that you served? Will you serve when there is no thank you, no progress, no gratitude, no plaque, no recognition?

Are you willing to be poured out like wine on the altar, past the wood, over the rocks, and onto the ground?

Continuities. If our willingness to make room for the world's vulnerable depends on our efficiency and success rate, most will not start, and many will not finish. Discipleship offers a more certain foundation on which to build.

WHAT DO YOU THINK?

1. Paul mentions numerous negative responses in the letter to the Philippians. Which would bother you the most?

2. Tell of a time you helped somebody and received no response or a negative reaction.

3. Why is it so difficult to continue to help when we seem to make no progress?

4. According to the author, Paul responded to the Philippians in three ways. Which of the three do you need to hear the most? Why?

28

PRACTICE PLAYING SECOND FIDDLE

Several years ago, Christian family expert Paul Faulkner wrote a book called *Achieving Success without Failing Your Family: How 30 Successful Families Achieved Family Excellence*.[1] He told stories of parents who soared in business, but also had wonderful families. One story took up Tim and Sherry. Tim was a top salesman who was a member of the millionaire's round table. In the story, they took an airliner on a family vacation. Once they arrived, Tim stopped by the restroom at the airport. After what seemed to be a long time, the family got worried. Then Tim reappeared. They asked, "What's wrong? Daddy, are you sick?" "No." "Why were you gone so long?"

"Nothing, really." They kept insisting, and finally he told them. Somebody had written a racist remark on the restroom wall. He found some cleanser and washed it off.

When our boys were in grade school, we were in the bleachers watching one of them play basketball. A young couple near us had a small baby. Suddenly, the child threw up all over the mother, itself, and the bleachers. People around her quickly scooted away.

---

[1] Paul Faulkner, *Achieving Success without Failing Your Family: How 30 Successful Families Achieved Family Excellence* (West Monroe, LA: Howard Books, 1994).

Nearby, a man, another father, got up, left, and came back shortly with wet paper towels from the restroom. He helped clean up the baby, the mother, and the bleachers. Then he crawled under the stands and cleaned up the floor.

I find those stories inspiring. I'm touched by those fathers, moved by their service, awed by their actions. But those stories raise questions: Why are people like that so noteworthy? Why do such simple acts make them stand out? Why, out of thousands of people in a major airport, did it take a member of the millionaire's club to clean up the trashy graffiti? Out of the hundreds there at the ball game, why did the father of a boy playing basketball rise to help?

As I think about those stories, I also feel shame. I see terrible things on restroom walls, and I never think to wash them off. I've been there when children got sick, but I seldom offered to help. What's the difference between those men and me? Why did Tim wash the airport restroom wall when I likely would not even have thought about it? Why am I one of those people scooting away from the odor of the baby's vomit?

I struggle with my own self-centeredness. I want to be clean, not get my hands dirty. I want to be comfortable, not down on my knees. I want to be safe, not vulnerable. I want to be entertained, and all this sounds like work. What do I need?

Romans 12 describes Tim and the man at the ball game. It challenges me to become more than I am. Verse 10 tells me to outdo others in showing honor. Verse 11 says never burn out doing good. Verse 13 calls me to contribute to the needs of others and open my home to the needy. Verse 14 asks me to do good to those who hurt me. Verse 15 says be happy with happy people and sad with those who are sad. Verse 16 urges me to make friends with nobodies. Verse 17 directs me to discover the beauty in others. Verse 20 challenges me to feed the hungry and give a drink to those who are thirsty, even if I spy one there who is my enemy.

That's the kind of man Paul Faulkner described in his book and the heart of the man in the grade-school gym. That's the kind of person I want to be—more concerned about others than about myself and not afraid to help those in need.

All of Romans revolves around the saving action of Jesus at the cross, to which we respond in faith. That's covered in Romans 1–11. Then Romans 12:1–3 gives a foundation for all those actions:

> I appeal to you therefore, brethren, by the mercies of God, to present your bodies as a living sacrifice, holy and acceptable to God, which is your spiritual worship. Do not be conformed to this world but be transformed by the renewal of your mind, that you may prove what is the will of God, what is good and acceptable and perfect. For by the grace given to me I bid every one among you not to think of himself more highly than he ought to think, but to think with sober judgment, each according to the measure of faith which God has assigned him.

Just as Jesus offered himself as my sacrifice, now he calls me to climb up on the altar with him and present my body, myself, my being, as a sacrifice to help him serve others. Then he mentions a negative and a positive.

First is the negative: don't think like the world. Don't think of yourself more highly than you ought. Don't misjudge your status in life. Left to our own devices, we get caught up in pride, arrogance, and superiority, or we drift into the stagnant and complacent life.

There are two ways of thinking: the world's way and God's way. A few years back, a teenager named Jeremy sexually molested and murdered a seven-year-old girl in a Las Vegas casino. I read about the incident in a long-forgotten Los Angeles newspaper. The reporter followed the story and learned that Jeremy's friend David witnessed the crime. He didn't try to stop it. He even refused to serve as a witness against his friend in court. The reporter asked David, "Why did you refuse?" David said, "I'm not going to get upset over someone else's life. I just worry about myself first."

Most of us don't say it, but many of us think that way. Because of Christ, we give up thinking like the world and we start thinking like Jesus. The Las Vegas David, like us, thought of himself more highly than he ought.

Second, the positive point out of Romans 12:1–3 calls us to think with sober judgment about what God has given us. Don't think of yourself as nothing. Don't think you can't make a difference. Don't think what you do doesn't matter.

Real life comes from God. We are not gods who created the earth; we are earthlings created by God. We are people who have taken up our cross and followed Jesus. We're not passengers on the cruise ship; we are crew members on a cargo ship. Our model is Jesus.

He came not to be served but to serve. He healed. He fed. He touched. He counseled. Finally, he died.

William Green was a professor at the University of California at Berkley and then later at Pepperdine University. He translated several volumes of the Harvard University Loeb Classical Library.[2] He was world famous as a model scholar.

Students remember him walking across campus holding the hand of his wife Ruby. A friend of mine, Billie Silvey, says that Dr. Green surprised her with a birthday party when her husband Frank was on military duty overseas. When he lived in Berkeley, he was an elder in the local Church of Christ. The other elder was a janitor at the same university. At noon, people knew that the two men would be in the janitor's broom closet praying and having lunch. Imagine a world-renowned classical scholar and a man with a broom sharing lunch in the back of the boiler room.

Don't think like the world. Don't let the world mold you into its way of thinking. Think soberly. As a person who has received grace from the servant Jesus, become a servant and pass the grace on to others.

Who knows, if we all move in the right direction, we may find ourselves working together to wash off the graffiti or wipe up the mess.

Continuities. Making room can call us to deal with something as odious as a racist comment on a bathroom wall or a baby's vomit at a basketball game. Sacrificing ourselves with Jesus may lead us to make room for lunch in the janitor's closet.

---

[2] For example: *Augustine: City of God*, Loeb Classical Library, Volume V, Books 16–18.35, trans. Eva M. Sanford and William M. Green (Cambridge, UK: Harvard University Press, 1965).

WHAT DO YOU THINK?

1. Romans 12:10–20 lists a series of commands. Which do you already do? Which have you never done? Which one could you do this week?

2. When it comes to service, list ways in which we often think like the world.

3. When it comes to service, list ways in which we can think like Christ.

4. Paul says we shouldn't be conformed to the world. In what way have you or other Christians conformed to the world's culture? What does Jesus specifically say about your area of conforming?

29

IF GOD BE FOR US, WHO CAN BE AGAINST US?

ROMANS 8:31

One critical moment in Jesus's ministry occurred in Matthew 16. Jesus and the disciples were visiting Caesarea Philippi when Jesus asked, "Who do men say that the Son of man is?" They provided a list: John the Baptist, Elijah, Jeremiah, or one of the prophets.

I've always wondered about that list. Why did they think Jesus had connections with John the Baptist or the prophets? Did they look alike, use the same words, or carry the same reputation? Let's just focus on one: Jeremiah.

Why did they think Jesus Christ was Jeremiah? Let me suggest three possible reasons.

First, the people knew a great deal about Jeremiah. The book of Jeremiah has the most words of any biblical book. His fifty-two chapters take up his ministry in the late seventh and early sixth centuries BC. Jeremiah was in prison in Jerusalem when the Babylonians set the city on fire. Jeremiah was nearby when Nebuchadnezzar's soldiers pulled down the temple stones.

Some scholars say we know more about Jeremiah than any other Old Testament character. Some say we know more about Jeremiah than any other person in the Bible aside from Jesus and Paul.

He's best known for his confessions. They were times when he poured out his heart to God and wrote them down for us to read.

Second, people thought Jesus was Jeremiah because of Jeremiah's faith. Jeremiah preached to people who didn't believe and would not listen. In a world of unfaithful people, Jeremiah stood out as a man of faith. He had doubts, complaints, and accusations, but he never gave up on faith.

Third, people thought Jesus was Jeremiah because of how the prophet did ministry. Whenever I've taught the book of Jeremiah, students come up afterward and say, "Thank you for introducing me to this book. I didn't know there was so much about how to do ministry in the Bible." Listen to some of the things Jeremiah said about ministry.

In Jeremiah 4:19, the prophet writes, "My anguish, my anguish! I writhe in pain! Oh, the walls of my heart! My heart is beating wildly; I cannot keep silent." It's one of the few examples of a possible heart attack in the Bible. Perhaps it's a cry of intense anxiety. Jeremiah saw the coming destruction of the city where he ministered and the ruin of the people that he served. As a result, what he saw filled him with anguish that they would not respond to his message. It's a classic case of the personal cost of ministry. Ministry is not something one does only with the mind and not the heart.

On another occasion, God warned Jeremiah, "Let everyone beware of his neighbor" and told him not to "trust in any brother." Then God tells Jeremiah, people we think of as brothers can be supplanters, slanderers, deceivers, sinners, people unwilling to repent, oppressors, and ultimately those who do not know God (Jer. 9:4–6). He told Jeremiah that the people in the pew can be deceitful. Even your own family can't be fully trusted. God described a dysfunctional society where most relationships are broken, trust has eroded, social networks are disrupted, and honesty is gone.

On another occasion, Jeremiah bared his soul. He, in effect, cried out, "What did I do wrong? I've never hurt these people, yet they curse me in the streets. I wish I'd never been born." It's a classic case of loneliness and isolation. Everybody is against me; nobody is for me (Jer. 15:10–11).

People made fun of Jeremiah, and he felt like a "laughingstock." When he warned them with his prophetic speeches, they ridiculed his words and told jokes about him. Jeremiah felt derided and reproached. He wanted to stop and give up. But he could not quit. The Word of God burned like a fire in his belly. He couldn't stop preaching (Jer. 20:7–9).

Finally, these sad words: "For twenty-three years, from the thirteenth year of Josiah the son of Amon, king of Judah, to this day, the word of the LORD has come to me, and I have spoken persistently to you, but you have not listened" (Jer. 25:3). Jeremiah preached in the same place for over two decades and had no conversions. Twenty-three years of offering the invitation with nobody coming forward. No baptisms, no responses, no restorations. From an efficiency point of view, Jeremiah gets an "F" in ministry.

Yet there is one great reality about Jeremiah the prophet. He was right. The kings of Judah were wrong. The people who made fun of him were wrong. The people who refused to listen were wrong. Today, about one billion people have a copy of his book and they carry it to church. The ministry of Jeremiah is held up as one of the greatest examples of service in world history.

I know Jeremiah is an old, complex, and generally unknown book to many. So, students of Jeremiah have tried to find a line to summarize the book. They seek a single line that wraps up his ministry in a brief statement. Maybe Paul's line summarizes Jeremiah's service: "If God is for us, who is against us?" (Rom. 8:31).

If God calls us to his work, it doesn't matter who opposes us. It doesn't matter that the Babylonian army gave the prophet a near heart attack, or that deception characterized their broken world, or that he felt alone because of the reproach of the people, or that Jeremiah got ridiculed for what he said, or that he preached twenty-three years without a response. It doesn't matter; because if God is for Jeremiah, it makes no difference who is against him.

How does that play out in our world? What does it mean to a contemporary preacher or a church leader or a Sunday school teacher or the director of VBS? The culture may send waves against us, we may sense the deception and brokenness of our own society, and we may feel isolated, ridiculed, and like failures. How do we go on?

First, keep on serving. The Word of God is more powerful than any force in any society. The most common phrase in the Bible's longest book from the pen of Jeremiah is "the Word of God." We are not the power; the Word of God is the power.

Second, don't let those around you dictate your life. Jeremiah lived in a negative, faithless environment, but that's not what dictated his service. Jeremiah kept in touch with God, and that made the difference.

Third, keep your heart focused on hope. Jeremiah wrote at one of history's darkest moments. Those lines in Jeremiah 30–33 are often called the Book of Comfort. Some of the Bible's most hopeful words are found in these four chapters. Jeremiah knew a better day was coming and that God would provide a better future.

Fourth, wait. Be persistent. Let God act in his own time. We can't imagine preaching twenty-three years without a conversion, but Jeremiah persevered. He knew God would create a new covenant and things would be different.

If God be for us, who can be against us? Jeremiah faced opposition from Israel in Jerusalem and from the Babylonians outside Jerusalem. He often thought he ministered with one arm tied behind his back. But he found that God turned his weakness into strength.

No wonder people thought that Jesus was Jeremiah.

Continuities. Making room means we need a model. Jeremiah's ministry modeled faithfulness to the one who called him to the mission. We do well to imitate him.

WHAT DO YOU THINK?

1. Which of the situations faced by Jeremiah would trouble you the most?

2. Describe a person you know who serves as Jeremiah served.

3. Discuss Jeremiah's line: "There is in my heart as it were a burning fire shut up in my bones, and I am weary with holding it in, and I cannot." What do you think he meant? Have you ever felt that way? How does that fire motivate service?

4. The author gives four suggestions to help us keep serving even when it is difficult with no response. Which of the four do you need to heed today? Why?

30

COURAGE TO BE DIFFERENT—CALL TO TOTAL COMMITMENT

ROMANS 12:1-5

Perpetua grew up in North Africa during the harsh years of the Roman Empire. As a young woman, she became a follower of Jesus. When she turned twenty-two, authorities put her in prison because of her faith. Twice, her father came to beg her to renounce Jesus. He belonged to a noble, well-connected, and wealthy family. But Perpetua loved Jesus, and she refused to reject him.

Finally, the Romans took Perpetua to the arena. The Christians did battle with the lions. One bloodied Perpetua. The crowd objected. They didn't want to see a woman die in the mouth of a wild beast. The authorities took her away, found an appropriate spot, and cut off her head.[1]

Perpetua's oft-told story stirs us. We admire her courage. We salute her high standards. We stand amazed at her total commitment. Her sacrifice moves us all.

But her story makes me wonder. What if those events happened now instead of then? What if Christians battled lions in the arenas here instead of there? What if it were my son instead of his daughter? What if it was me and not her?

---

[1] Cited in Herbert Anthony Musurillo, *The Acts of the Christian Martyrs* (Oxford: Oxford University Press, 1972), 106–31.

What would I have done? Would I have gone to the prison intent on convincing my son to give up on Jesus for the sake of his life? Would I have pleaded with him to change his mind? Would I have renounced my Lord? How am I so different from her?

During one of the wars in the Middle East, young people feared that U.S. troops would be deployed to the scene of the battles. A reporter interviewed students from an Ivy League university. One student said that the people in Afghanistan were not worth dying for. Then he added something like, "I don't believe there is anything worth dying for."[2]

Secretly, many of us agree. But as we ponder that statement, we realize we all die. We die for something, or we die for nothing. We stand for something, or we stand for nothing.

Romans 12:1–2 troubles us on this same issue. Paul tells us to "present your bodies as a living sacrifice." Such a sacrifice becomes our "spiritual worship." By this sacrifice, we refuse to "be conformed to this world," but instead we are "transformed by the renewal of your mind."

Sacrifice means death. We think of animals cut up and burned on the altar. We recall how Cain and Abel offered their sacrifices. Noah left the ark to light the fire and offer the sacrifice. On and on it goes: Abraham at Shechem, Jacob at Bethel, Moses at the tabernacle, Solomon at the temple.

But Romans 12 brings us back to Perpetua. It recalls all those martyred for Jesus. David Barrett claims that a third of a million people die each year due to their faith.[3] It brings up the question: Am I willing to be a sacrifice?

Romans 12 sets high expectations. It raises the standard. It's a call for total commitment. What does it mean? The two images in the passage guide us.

The first image arises out of Romans 1–11. Imagine a pile of stones with wood on top with a fire burning. People stand around in anticipation. Lambs and cows wait in nearby pens. It's the altar of burnt offerings. The rocks are stained red.

Then two men approach. One is God the Father, the other Jesus the Son. God puts Jesus on top of the fire. He offers him as a sacrifice.

---

[2] Stanley Hauerwas and William H. Willimon, *Resident Aliens* (Nashville: Abingdon, 1989), 149–50.

[3] David Barrett, *Evangelize: A Historical Survey of the Concept* (Birmingham: New Hope, 1987).

If one image dominates Romans 1–11, this is it. *I'm not ashamed of the gospel.* I'm not ashamed of the sacrifice. All have sinned and fall short of the glory of God. It takes a sacrifice to right that wrong. While we were yet sinners, Jesus died for us. Jesus was sacrificed for us. By his sacrifice, he frees us from sin, clears the way so we can be friends with him, and pays the penalty we owed. Image one: Jesus on the altar.

The second image reflects Romans 12–16. It's the same pile of rocks and the same wood and fire. The same people mill around next to the animals inside the fences. Jesus is on top of the altar. God stands nearby. Then he approaches each one of us. He tells us to crawl up on the altar with Jesus. I obey and put my body on the fire as a living sacrifice. I crawl up on the back of Jesus.

It makes me a living sacrifice. Animals died on the altar. This living sacrifice goes on sacrificing. It's a way of life.

It makes me a holy sacrifice. Not holy in the sense of being good enough, but in the sense that my life is set aside for God's purposes. We don't just sacrifice our hand and keep everything else. We throw our whole body on the fire.

It makes me an acceptable sacrifice. That means by this action I please God; not the world, not my family, not myself, but my Lord.

God sacrificed Jesus for us. Then he calls us to sacrifice ourselves for him. Once we climb on the altar, our life belongs to him. We put ourselves into the fire. We become a living sacrifice, giving our whole life to please him.

We give up looking at church and Christianity with the question, "What's in it for me?" We give up saying, "I didn't get much out of that sermon." We stop saying, "I'll let somebody else do it." We cease making spiritual decisions based on whether we're comfortable or not. When God calls, we refuse to say, "I'm too busy."

Paul Laurence Dunbar was the son of a former slave. Dunbar operated an elevator, but wrote poetry during his off hours. He knew something of being a living sacrifice. Out of that belief, he wrote the poem "Too Busy." In the first verse of the poem, Dunbar writes, "the Lord had a job for me," but he excuses himself, saying that he is too busy with his own business to do what the Lord needs. In the second verse, the roles are reversed; Dunbar desperately needs the Lord to help him. Yet Dunbar hears only silence from the Lord. Dunbar interprets the silence as the Lord responding to him the way he himself had responded, as if the Lord, too, was busy and Dunbar would have to wait. The final verse shows Dunbar reflecting on how he has changed since then. He now stops what he is doing to do the Lord's work as soon as he is asked, because there is no one else who can do what "God's marked out for you."[4]

Crawl up on the altar with Jesus and be a living sacrifice for him.

Continuities. I cannot think of a more graphic illustration of the status of the person willing to listen and make room than the image of the disciple of Christ crawling up on the altar to be a living sacrifice with Jesus.

WHAT DO YOU THINK?

1. How do you respond to the story of Perpetua? What do you like about it? What do you not like?

2. Discuss Romans 12:1. How does it summarize Romans 1–11? How does it relate to Romans 12–16?

3. What does "presenting our bodies as a living sacrifice" look like in today's world? Give examples you have observed.

4. Have you ever thought like Paul Laurence Dunbar? What changed his mind? What might change your mind?

---

[4] Paul Laurence Dunbar, *The Collected Poetry of Paul Laurence Dunbar*, ed. Joanne M. Braxton (Charlottesville: University of Virginia Press, 1993), 344.

31

DON'T CUT CORNERS

MATTHEW 7:13-14

They call it the Sermon on the Mount. It contains some of the most famous lines Jesus ever said:

- "Blessed are the poor in spirit, for theirs is the kingdom of heaven" (Matt. 5:3).
- "Let your light so shine before men, that they may see your good works and give glory to your Father who is in heaven" (Matt. 5:16).
- "But seek first his kingdom and his righteousness, and all these things shall be yours as well" (Matt. 6:33).
- "So whatever you wish that men would do to you, do so to them" (Matt. 7:12).

The teaching of Matthew 5–7 falls into three categories. First, we must have the right attitude. Nine beatitudes lead the way. Keeping the right attitude means not giving in to worry. Second, we are called to adopt his moral standards. Do not kill or even hate. Do not commit adultery or even lust. Make your yes a yes. Morality is acting the right way. Third, we must imitate his piety. Ask and you will receive. Seek and you will find. Knock and the door will be opened for you. Piety is drawing close to God.

The hinge of the sermon comes after the Golden Rule in Matthew 7:12. Jesus changed focus from what we are to do to the cost of following him.

He told us how to live, now he tells us what it will take. He did it with four sets of two.

First, there are two gates: a wide one and a narrow one. The wide gate is easy to navigate. Getting through the gate is simple. There are no security checks, no baggage limit, and no restrictions. You don't have to leave anything behind. You can pack your bag full of bad attitudes, immoral actions, poor decisions, and lack of piety, and they'll let you in.

The narrow gate offers restrictions. It's hard to find, easy to miss, and once you are there, it's difficult to get through. They search everything when you come to this gate. All the past baggage has to be left outside.

Second, there are two roads: one is easy, the other is hard. The easy road has multiple lanes; every lane is wide, spacious, and roomy. You can drive in the lane you choose or even in two at the same time. Follow your whims. You can travel this road with your hands in your pockets.

The other road is hard. It twists and turns, gets narrow and bumpy. Most find it difficult to travel and find little comfort in the trip. It takes effort, sweat, and late nights.

Third, there are two groups of people: the many and the few. The many describes a scene of wall-to-wall people. You never get to be alone with this group. You flow with the crowd. It's like shopping at Christmas or the concession stand at halftime.

The other group includes just a few. Not many people join this group. At times, it seems like you travel alone. You can't see anybody in front of you or behind you.

Fourth, there are two destinations. Jesus called one destination destruction and the other one life. Jesus didn't call destruction hell, but it doesn't sound any better. The wide road comes to an abrupt end. The luggage never arrives when you do. The end is labeled frustration and the trade name is disappointment.

Jesus labeled the other destination life. He didn't call it heaven, but life is clearly a place worth going. The sad find comfort. The pure in heart see God. Those in the kingdom business see the king.

The point that runs through the four sets of two is a call to discipline. A life worth living doesn't come by taking shortcuts. Brilliant faith is not a part-time job. Jesus wants our full attention. He draws a line in the sand and calls us to be disciples.

William Boggs, in his book *Sin Boldly: But Trust God More Boldly Still*, tells of taking an afternoon drive in the Carolinas when he saw a sign advertising "Peaches for Sale." The line below said, "Pick them yourself." He decided to do it. The old man running the orchard said if you want the best peaches, go deep into the orchard. Most people picked over the peaches on the edges. Boggs thought it was a good idea. He walked some distance into the orchard and started to pick some fruit. The old man cried out, "Go deeper." Boggs walked further and stopped. The voice urged, "Go deeper." He walked even further and set the basket down, but the old man shouted, "Go deeper." So Boggs walked substantially further. Surely this was far enough. The distant voice said, "Go deeper." Boggs continued to walk. He found out the farmer was right. The finest, plumpest peaches were untouched, waiting for him.[1]

Jesus talked about roads, Boggs about peaches, but the point is the same. Go deeper. The narrowest gate, the hardest road, the smaller crowd, the more distant destination offers the deepest satisfaction.

We often miss out on the best in life because we pick the closest road. Going deeper means turning off the TV, laying aside the phone, ignoring the racy movies, setting aside an addiction to social media, loving the hard to love, giving to the beggar, and rising above pettiness. It means listening and making room.

My son Nathan had a fifth-grade teacher who asked the children to write to a grandparent and ask about what the world was like when they were ten. Nathan wrote to Sally's dad, Wayne Tague. Nathan got back a two-page letter describing life in Iowa ninety years before. There was one striking paragraph:

> Our little country church house was down the road a mile.
> There was no air conditioning for the hot summer weather. On
> Sunday, one of the men would go early and open all the win-
> dows to cool down the building somewhat. In the winter, during

---

[1] William Boggs, *Sin Boldly: But Trust God More Boldly Still* (Nashville: Abingdon Press, 1990), 101–2.

the real cold days, someone would volunteer to go early and build a fire in the big stove, but even then, we could sometimes see the breath come out of the preacher's mouth. In those years, there were no excuses for staying home on Sunday, no matter how hot or cold the outside temperatures.

We all know the late 1920s was not a perfect age. They had issues with integrity and morality. There were family problems and their versions of selfishness and pettiness. But memory helps us see the choice between the two roads with greater clarity.

It makes me rethink my responses. When I think of somebody doing something I don't like, I think of the farmer walking miles in the snow to light the fire for the church. When somebody gets me down, I remember the teenager getting up at 5:30 A.M. to air out the church building in western Iowa. When things don't go my way, I visualize the man with thorns on his head walking down the narrow road, and that sets me right. When I get my feelings hurt, nothing changes me more than seeing the blood and water running out of his side.

All of the work of discipline comes under the umbrella of grace. We don't get to heaven because we choose the narrow gate, walk the hard road by ourselves, or seek the little-found destination of life. We arrive by the grace and mercy of God.

Once, I read about a monastery the Franciscans built in the 1500s northwest of Madrid, Spain. The Spanish king hired an architect to design the structure, and he incorporated a set of arches that were flat on the top. When the king saw the arches, he was afraid they would fall, so he instructed the architect to erect pillars in the center of each arch to support them. The architect protested but complied.

Years later, the king died. The architect revealed that the pillars were a quarter inch short of touching the bottom of the arch. Even today, tour guides slide a piece of paper between the top of the pillar and the bottom of the arches. In five centuries it hasn't sagged at all.[2]

---

[2] David H. Roper, "Praise, Poise, and Prayer," Discovery Publishing, No. 3042 (September 3, 1972), http://ldolphin.org/roper/rejoicing/3042.html.

God builds an arch over our lives. We may think we have to keep those arches from sagging. Our task is to keep our eyes on the God who holds up the arch. Every day is a journey. We choose between two gates. We take one of two roads. We travel with one of two crowds. We head to one of two destinations. Our choices make all the difference.

> **Continuities.** Jesus lays out the choices before us. In the broader context, it is a choice between listening to the vulnerable and not listening. It is a decision between making room and not making room. The task before us calls for discipline.

WHAT DO YOU THINK?

1. What is the point Jesus makes in his four sets of twos? Which do you find the most convicting?

2. Share a time when you chose the narrow gate or the hard road. What was the result?

3. The author says that making the hard choices leads to greater satisfaction. Do you agree or disagree?

4. Why does it take discipline to listen and make room?

5. Discuss the relationship between discipline and grace.

32

MERCY!

LUKE 6:32-36

Five of us gathered for a buffet dinner. There were two married couples and a teenager named Terry. She wasn't related to any of us. I tried to engage Terry in conversation, but she never responded. I wondered why she would not answer my questions. I couldn't understand why she avoided eye contact. She never said a word.

After dinner, when Terry had gone, I learned her story. She'd been attacked by a group of men. They did all the things you most fear. They left her helpless, beaten, and violated.

The next event was almost as bad as the first. Her family refused to let her come home. They blamed her. They told her she should be ashamed. When she reached out for security, comfort, and home, she got accusations, rejection, and pain.

Terry was bent and broken. Then she encountered a wonderful Christian couple named Randy and Kim. Their own children were in their twenties and away at school. Randy and Kim invited Terry to stay in their guest room. Terry moved in. She was at the buffet because she knew Randy and Kim. She had done more than move into their house, she had moved into their hearts.

They listened and made room. They tended to her bent and broken situation. They offered comfort after the terrible attack. They welcomed a girl rejected by her biological family into their family. They accepted her, showed her honor, and gave her security.

People like Terry are all around us. We encounter them—the bent, pressured, tense, broken, raw without anywhere to turn.

Luke 6 is a rough parallel to Terry's story. Jesus arrived at a "level place" where a substantial audience gathered from locations near and far. Some had diseases, others were "troubled with unclean spirits," but everyone found healing in Jesus (Luke 6:17–19). Many in the crowd were like Terry. They were sick, troubled, bent, and nearly broken. All that was good and wonderful in their lives had been taken away.

Jesus addressed their needs, but then gave them a bigger picture. "Blessed are you poor, for yours is the kingdom of God." The poor thought they owned nothing, but Jesus made them citizens of the kingdom. He continued, "Blessed are you that hunger now, for you shall be satisfied." Those hungry people felt like nobodies. Jesus said they were somebodies on the way to a better life. "Blessed are you when men hate you." Others might exclude them, but Jesus took them in. To those who were the selfish rich, who refused to share what they ate, who laughed at the poor, and who sought to be admired, Jesus offered no such hope (Luke 6:20–26).

He blessed the poor, the hungry, the weeping, and the hated. He took to task the rich, the full, the mockers, and the popular. Jesus knew about the bent and nearly broken.

He went on to tell them how to respond to their oppressors. He listed the wrongdoers: the enemy, the haters, cursers, abusers, strikers, beggars, cons, and the thieves. He told the hurting to respond in love, do what they don't expect, give love to people who cannot give it to you.

Then he reached the heart of the matter in verses 35–36. Jesus said when we show mercy, we are children of God. When we show mercy, we become like our heavenly Father. Mercy doesn't come from our own resources, from our own bentness, from the way others treat us, or from the culture around us. It comes from the heart of God.

What's going on in these twenty verses? Jesus spoke to the bent and broken. He pronounced blessings and woes. Then he called them to live for the sake of a higher cause. He rooted it all in the heart of his Father, the great champion of mercy.

It's a celebration of mercy. He made mercy central to life. He called mercy the heartbeat of the church. He revealed mercy as the standard of

God and said we should make it our practice. He pointed out the people who are like the Father.

In a world that celebrates only the powerful and the beautiful, Jesus celebrated the unlovable. In a world that lauds the ambitious and those at the top, Jesus elevated the servants. Those who stood at the end of the line, Jesus moved to the front of the line. Those who work for the vulnerable get lauded. In a world that can't get past the glamour and the exterior, Jesus ministered to the unglamorous and the fractured. He said it is not about me; it's about the Father.

Jesus wanted children to grow up seeing mercy championed, attending churches where the most soiled human beings can find home, where no flame—no matter how weak—is ever put out, where the goal of all the people all the time in all things no matter what the cost is to be merciful as the Father is merciful.

E. H. Ijams was one of my mentors in ministry. Ijams played the same role for Landon Saunders. One day, Landon told me that Ijams had a gentle spirit and didn't want to hurt people who held views he didn't agree with. He never pulled rank. He never used power. Then Landon said, "The result was that the weakest, most stained, most soiled human being could sit in the presence of E. H. Ijams in total safety. They would not be attacked or torn down. He would not put out the weakest flame."

When I heard that, I was deeply moved. That's the kind of man I want to be. That's the kind of person I want to be around. That's the kind of man I want my sons to be. That's the kind of person I want to go to church with. That kind of man is in the image of the Father.

I want to join Jesus in the celebration of mercy. Let's celebrate those whose service is unseen, who sit by bedsides in hospitals, who mow lawns of widows without pay, who run errands for shut-ins, who encourage people who never encourage them, who give huge amounts of money anonymously, who hold the hands of the grieving, who let themselves be run over for the sake of a bigger cause.

Let's celebrate those who cradle babies they did not birth, who clean up the vomit of a child not their own, who stay up all night with a foster kid, who go to court repeatedly to get justice for a five-year-old, who plead with the bureaucrats to pay more attention to children than the budget, who beg people for money to take care of the unwanted, and who talk through the night to the teen who wants to abort.

Let's celebrate! Let's be merciful as our Father in heaven is merciful.

Continuities. Nothing makes us listen and make room for the world's most vulnerable more than mercy.

WHAT DO YOU THINK?

1. Describe somebody you know like Randy and Kim, who showed mercy to a vulnerable person.

2. List ten ways you could show mercy this week. Pick three and commit to doing them.

3. How does showing mercy make us like God?

4. How can you be like E. H. Ijams and inspire others to be merciful?

5. In what ways have you been shown mercy?

33

LIFE!

MATTHEW 10:29-30

The human head typically has about eighty thousand hairs. Redheads have the least. Brown-haired and black-headed people often have over one hundred thousand hairs. Blondes have the most, with one hundred twenty thousand hairs.

Under normal conditions, we lose about one hundred hairs a day. As we look around, we see that some are well above average in that category.

The Gospels tell us that God has numbered our hairs. Keeping a census of hair sounds like it's out of the question. People who first heard that might have wondered why God would want to do a hair census. With all the digital equipment around us, keeping an inventory of hair might be much easier to do. Our wristband might blink and say, "Hair #475 just fell out." We could get a monthly printout of which ones we lost.

Matthew 10:29–30 puts it this way: "Are not two sparrows sold for a penny? And not one of them will fall to the ground without your Father's will. But even the hairs of your head are all numbered." Jesus spoke of two images: birds and hair. Neither a lone common sparrow nor a single strand of hair has much value in our culture. It didn't in theirs either. Yet we see the point. If God keeps track of these throwaway items and values them, how much more must he value us?

We can only imagine Jesus visiting the room in heaven where God keeps track of human hair. Standing off to the side, Jesus watches his Father counting every hair on every human head. It means he knows when we're drowning in a sea of confusion, or when we're afraid for our children, or when we're concerned about a family problem, or when we're on a path to nowhere.

Jesus followed up that image with one of his last promises while on earth. After telling the disciples to go into all the world, he promised, "Lo, I am with you always, to the close of the age" (Matt. 28:20). He's always at our side. There's never a moment when he's gone.

We get echoes of this thought elsewhere. Whenever two or three of you gather, I'll be in your midst (Matt. 18:20). He told Paul, "I am with you, and no man shall attack you to harm you; for I have many people in this city" (Acts 18:10). If we love God, he is there to make sure all things work together for good. Nothing can stand in the way of his love (Rom. 8:28, 31).

In the struggles of life, Jesus sides with us. Despite the way it might look, the end turns out good. If God is on my side, it doesn't really matter who's on the other side. God stands at our side in power and victory.

Yet we all have moments when we think we don't matter and when we feel all alone. We'd like a sign from heaven that affirms God knows we're here. We generally don't get the signs we want, but in Scripture, we have the written guarantee. In fact, the testimony of millions of Christians from the past and present affirms the promises are trustworthy.

Ravi Zacharias speaks widely on college campuses. I heard him speak about his friend Hien. They met in Vietnam in the early 1970s. Hien was a Christian and Ravi's translator. Suddenly, Hien disappeared. They didn't reconnect until 1988.

When Vietnam fell, the Vietcong arrested all the Vietnamese connected to Americans. Since Hien had worked for the U.S. Army as translator, he was among the first arrested. While he was imprisoned, they pressured him to adopt the teachings of Marx and Engels. It was mental torture for months on end. Hien finally broke under the pressure. He could no longer believe in a God who allowed him to go through such torture. One day, he decided, If I'm not freed tomorrow, I give up on God.

It no longer mattered that God said he had Hien's hairs numbered. Jesus wasn't in prison with him. All things were not working for good. He woke the next morning, and for the first time in years, he didn't pray. That exact day, the prison commander assigned him to clean the officer's latrine. The conditions were revolting. He could hardly stand it, but he did his work. As he emptied the latrine wastebasket, he noticed a piece of used toilet paper. The toilet paper had writing on it. It was in English. It had been a long time since he had read English, so he wiped the toilet paper clean. He slipped it into his pocket and finished his work.

Late that night while in the privacy of his bed, he pulled out what had been toilet paper. As the others slept, he moved the paper to the light. The paper he fished out of the trash can was just the corner of a page. It had these words on it. "All things work together for good to those that love the Lord. Nothing can separate you from the love of God."

Hien volunteered to clean the officer's latrine every day, and he did so. A missionary had given the commander a Bible. He used it as toilet paper. Hien collected nearly the entire book of Romans. Later, he escaped from prison and settled in California.[1]

Hien's story is not proof. It's just one man in a long line of Christians who claim the assurances. They testify to the fact that God counts hairs. God is with us. All things work for the good. Nothing can separate us from the love of God.

I visited Papua New Guinea in September of 2004. I was to speak to about 150 people at the graduation ceremony at Melanesian Bible College. It sits at the edge of the jungle in a primitive country where the people speak eight hundred different languages. Pidgin English is the national language. Most of the people at graduation had walked through the jungle for nearly a week to attend. They forded streams, slept in the rain forest, and lived off the land.

The prospect of making the speech frightened me. I'd never spoken to people in that setting before. What should I say? How could I connect? My translator was a tall Papua New Guinean named Jab. The pulpit was a tree complete with roots that had been yanked out of the forest and cut off at an angle waist high.

I finally decided to take three lines from a story of Jesus and to use those words to make some points. I started into the lesson. The audience

---

[1] Randy Mosier, "The Story of Hien Pham, as Told by Ravi Zacharias," *Tools for Christian Living* (blog), September 22, 2017, https://toolsforchristianliving.wordpress.com/2017/09/22/the-story-of-hien-pham-as-told-by-ravi-zacharias/.

seemed distracted. People were not listening. Some were going to sleep. For some reason, I wasn't connecting.

So in the middle of the speech, I changed directions. In all the lessons I had given in my decades of preaching, I'd never switched topics so abruptly. It suddenly came to me that I should tell the story of my conversion. I moved from what I had prepared to my own story. I told it anonymously. I told about a little boy searching for God. He didn't know where to find God. He met a woman who grew potatoes. She told him about God and invited him over to her house for dinner. Finally, she told him about the God who loved him.

After telling the little boy's story, I said this line:

"That little boy was me."

I waited for Jab to translate. He said nothing. I looked over at him. He was crying. I didn't know what to do. It was the key line of my story. I thought, *My speech is ruined.*

Then I realized it was out of my hands. I had reached the end of my ability. The God who had promised to be with me was there at that critical moment. All things were working for good.

Suddenly, 150 people began to clap. Many were crying. They wiped away tears. They got the message even though Jab never translated that line.

That's not proof. It's just one person's experience in a long line of people who claim the assurances of God. We give testimony to the fact that God counts hairs and that in him, all things work together for good.

Even when you're cleaning a prison latrine or off in the jungle out of your element, even when you feel life is out of control, he's there working all things for good.

Continuities. Being a disciple can be lonely business, and making room for the vulnerable people around us may isolate us from others. Not everybody is lining up to listen and make room. In the end, it doesn't matter, because God is always at our side. We are not alone.

WHAT DO YOU THINK?

1. What is the point of Jesus's illustration about human hair?

2. How did you respond to the story told by Ravi Zacharias?

3. Share a time when you did not think God was working for the good in your life.

4. How do you think vulnerable children in your city would respond if you told them God was working for good in their lives?

5. The author shares his experience of God being with him at a critical moment. Share your own experience of God's presence in your life.

34

NOW IT DWELLS IN YOU
A MIGHTY PURPOSE

2 TIMOTHY 1:3

Most people have not heard of Jim Grant. A World War II veteran, Grant was born in China, moved to the United States, and died in January 1995. His biographers call him "an apostle of sorts, a crusader for children." He ran UNICEF, the United Nations International Children's Emergency Fund, from 1980 to 1995. One authority wrote that Grant was the "most powerful advocate for children the world has ever seen."

In 1982, some forty-six thousand children each day died from starvation, dirty water, and curable diseases. That's seventeen million children per year, or two thousand children per hour for every hour of the year. Grant launched a child survival revolution with a goal of vaccinating every child in the world against basic diseases by 1990. By that year, 80 percent of the world's children had the vaccination, including children in the world's poorest countries. The vaccination rate in India went from 6 percent of the children to 70 percent. In order to achieve that goal, Grant stopped wars, dealt with dictators, and raised money. It's estimated he saved the lives of three million children every year he served in the United Nations. They titled his biography, which reports this information, *A Mighty Purpose.*[1]

---

[1] Adam Fifield, *A Mighty Purpose: How Jim Grant Sold the World on Saving Its Children* (New York: Other Press, 2015).

It's a striking story about a man who saved the lives of more children than anybody in history, who reduced the number of children's deaths from forty-six thousand per day to seventeen thousand per day, and who risked his own life to protect the lives of children.

It made me wonder. Why has nobody risen to take his place? How does his effort to go into the entire world reflect on the Great Commission of Jesus? Are there any people as concerned about saving the spiritual lives of children as Jim Grant was about saving their physical lives? What is our "mighty purpose?" Do we have any Jim Grants in the church today?

The first place to turn to is the Bible.

In Genesis 18:1–15, Abraham entertained three guests at his desert tent. One was God himself. After the meal and the announcement of the birth of Abraham and Sarah's son, God continued on to visit Sodom and Gomorrah. He wondered if he should keep his mission a secret from Abraham. Then in Genesis 18:19 he decided, "No, for I have chosen him, that he may charge his children and his household after him to keep the way of the LORD by doing righteousness and justice; so that the LORD may bring to Abraham what he has promised him." God gave Abraham a mighty purpose that centered on children. He didn't want events in Sodom and Gomorrah to distract Abraham from his mission to children. In effect, the first champion for children in the Bible is God.

In Deuteronomy 4:9–10, Moses spoke to Israel on the eve of the invasion of the Promised Land. He recalled events in the wilderness at Sinai and told them not to forget, but to pass those precious words on to their children and grandchildren. In the entire book of Deuteronomy, Moses never forgot the importance of saving the children.

When we think of Sinai, we recall the Ten Commandments, the smoke on the mountain, and the golden calf. Moses remembered that Sinai was about children, the children of the coming generations. What happened at the mountain was important for children. Moses was a champion for children.

Much of Proverbs centers on children. There's advice about morality, money management, perseverance, language, and alcohol. Then come these remarkable words: "Train up a child in the way he should go, and when he is old he will not depart from it" (Prov. 22:6). Communities need to know how to raise healthy and satisfied children. Solomon and the other authors of Proverbs were champions for children.

Most of Paul's epistles have a practical section. In Ephesians and Colossians, the practical part centers on the household codes. Here, he explained how the doctrine of Christianity should play out in the home: "Fathers, do not provoke your children to anger, but bring them up in the discipline and instruction of the Lord" (Eph. 6:4). Paul, a single man, recognized that fathers play a critical role in rearing children. Paul was another champion for children.

The last one I want to mention is the most unusual. Timothy grew up in Lystra as the son of a Jewish mother and a Greek father. Later, he joined Paul's team. Paul called him a coworker (Rom. 16:21), a brother (2 Cor. 1:1), a loyal child (1 Tim. 1:2), and a son (2 Tim. 2:1). They had a personal and a professional relationship. But Paul didn't raise Timothy. He recalled Timothy's "sincere faith," which came from his grandmother Lois and his mother Eunice (2 Tim. 1:2–5). Paul urged him to "continue in what you have learned," adding that "from childhood you have been acquainted with the sacred writings" (2 Tim. 3:14–15).

Timothy became a famous associate of Paul, but he learned faith as a child from his grandmother and his mother. Paul pointed to two more champions for children: Eunice and Lois. So the Bible overflows with champions for children.

God gives the task to Abraham outside Sodom and Gomorrah. Moses passes it on to Israel at Sinai. Solomon gives the mission to adults in the wisdom literature. Paul calls the church to be champions for children. Eunice and Lois championed one child who then touched thousands. The work of the champions of children did not end in the Bible. It goes on.

Mary Crozier died in 2015. She taught children in Sunday school at the Norvel Park Church of Christ in Zanesville, Ohio, for forty-eight years. She had no biological children of her own, but she had a higher purpose in being a champion for children.

Joyce McBride had one central project in her life. She taught four-year-olds. Before her death in 2015, she had taught 120 four-year-old children in her class at the Memorial Road Church of Christ in Oklahoma City. A thousand people came to her funeral. At one point during the service, they asked anybody who had been in her class to come to the platform. Hundreds went to the front. Then, standing before the funeral crowd, they recited Psalm 23 in unison. They had learned it as four-year-olds in the class of one of God's champions for children.

Mildred Stutzman taught the sixth graders at East Pike Church of Christ in Indiana, Pennsylvania. She and her husband Guy were farmers. She loved to find children who did not go to church and invite them to her class and to use her own money to send them to Christian camp. One summer, a boy who lived seven houses from the church building came to her VBS class. She taught him and his sisters about God. One of the girls is Bonnie Young, whose husband Dennis is a deacon at the Twenty-Sixth Street Church of Christ in Huntington, West Virginia. The boy she taught in sixth grade was me.

What's the point? All of these are regular people: farmers, wives, home-makers, and factory workers. But they invested in children and they made a difference. Like Abraham, Moses, Solomon, Paul, Eunice, and Lois, there are people today like Mary Crozier, Joyce McBride, and Mildred Stutzman who follow in their footsteps as champions of children.

We in America have a special connection to one of these champions. Eunice and Lois taught one child. Paul continued to mentor Timothy. Of all the early apostles and preachers, these two, Paul and Timothy, went to Europe. The descendants of those they led to Christ in Europe later went to America. In a sense, we Americans are Christians because Eunice and Lois taught a child.

Jim Grant sparked a revolution in the health of children, but God's people are part of a greater revolution. There are Jim Grants in the church. I hope there will always be men and women like him who are champions for children. The key question that remains is this: Are you one of them?

Continuities. In many ways, this chapter is autobiographical. I try to be a champion for vulnerable children. Somebody has to stand up repeatedly and say, Will you listen and make room? Champions keep the mission alive.

WHAT DO YOU THINK?

1. Which champion for children mentioned in the Bible most inspires you?

2. Name other people in the Bible who were champions for children.

3. Describe somebody you know who focused on helping and teaching children. Tell their story.

4. Make a list of ways in which you could listen and make room for children around the world and in your own neighborhood. Decide which ones you can do this month.

5. Was somebody a champion for you when you were young? Who and how?

35

THE ROAD TO SUNDAY MORNING CHURCH

DIRECTIONS FROM JAMES 1:27

The chapters in this book originated at a yearly conference of a group called Network 1:27. The name refers to three biblical texts: Genesis 1:27, 1 Samuel 1:27, and James 1:27. All three texts speak of the value of children. In many ways, the passage in James summarizes the message of this book. This chapter, longer than the others, seeks to understand the context and meaning of that one verse in James.

An Orphan Text

The best-known passage about orphans, widows, and pure religion may be James 1:27: "Religion that is pure and undefiled before God and the Father is this: to visit orphans and widows in their affliction, and to keep oneself unstained from the world." Numerous citations of this passage tend to use it without much concern for why James made this incredible statement or how it fits into his book. It becomes a kind of orphan text. Yet looking at the broader context of this passage makes this strong claim about pure religion even more striking. Linking pure religion, orphans, and widows first to its immediate setting, second to its role in the book of James, and third to how it fits in the flow of the entire Bible moves the power of this passage to a whole new level.

Pure Religion

The immediate context of James 1:27 is about religion and worship. The chapter and verse divisions in the Bible are not inspired, and here the separation between chapters one and two of James may create more distance than the author intended. James 2:1–13 (especially verses 2–4) may be the longest description in the New Testament of the early church gathered in assembly for worship. James actually described an event that took place just as the service began. He looked at where people sat, what people wore to church, and how beloved brothers and sisters made distinctions among those gathered for worship. He urged them to welcome the poor man into their worship assembly.

In this passage, James raised issues about church and the Christian life that go beyond our favorite pew, our preferred dress, and our interactions with other worshippers. As we take the road to church every Sunday, we might think about how our encounter with the little book of James affects how we view church and worship.

James's comments on religion and worship actually start in the verses before James 2:1–13. The section begins: "If anyone thinks he is religious, and does not bridle his tongue but deceives his heart, this man's religion is vain" (James 1:26). Thus, James takes up a series of comments on what it means to be "religious." It includes *self-identity* ("thinks he is religious"), *speech* ("bridle his tongue"), *potential failure* ("religion is vain"), treatment of the *vulnerable* ("orphans and widows in their afflictions"), relationship with the *world* ("unstained"), and behavior at the Sunday *assembly* ("show no partiality"). Thus, James links "religion" with the taking care of the vulnerable and Sunday assembly.

Regardless of where we come down on the issues of seating in the church auditorium, or what people wear to the assembly, or to distinctions we make in our worship, all agree that we should seek "pure and undefiled" religion. We seek excellence in religion. We want to do religion right. James puts all this talk of religion in the context of being "unstained from the world." That connection with the concept of *world* leads us to consider the whole book of James.

The Point of the Book of James

In popular usage, James often gets put into one of two boxes. First, James becomes a counterpoint to Paul. James's description of works balances Paul's emphasis on grace. The verses from Paul and James line up in point–counterpoint fashion, such as the ones below. This approach makes James stress the action side of the Christian faith.

Point-Counterpoint—Paul and James

For by grace you have been saved through faith; and this is not your own doing, it is the gift of God—not because of works, lest any man should boast. (Eph. 2:8–9)

But some one will say, "You have faith and I have works." Show me your faith apart from your works, and I by my works will show you my faith. You believe that God is one; you do well. Even the demons believe—and shudder. (James 2:18–19)

• •

Second, some serious students of the book of James say James has no sustained point. People often call James the "New Testament Book of Proverbs"; that is, like Proverbs, James often shifts topics. After all, the book features fifty-four illustrations and forty-five commands. How can we find continuity with so much diversity? Such a conclusion seems to release us from any search for an overarching message from the book.

Illustrations in the Book of James

1:6	doubts like waves of sea
1:10	riches are like flowers
1:12	heaven compared to a crown
1:15	sin compared to birth and growth
1:17	God compared to light
1:18	Christians are like firstfruits
1:23	a forgetful man and a mirror
1:26	the tongue is like a wild animal that needs a bridle
1:27	Christian living compared to cleanliness
2:2–7	partiality compared to rich and poor visitors to assembly
2:15–17	faith shown by helping ill-clad and hungry
2:19	faith without works compared to demons
2:20	faith without works is like a barren woman
2:21	faith without works is like Abraham in Gen. 22
2:25	faith without works is like Rahab in Josh. 2
2:26	faith without works is like body without spirit
3:2	mistakes compared to being bridled

3:3	bit in our mouth is like bit in horse's mouth
3:4	small rudder guides ship like the small tongue controls the body
3:5	small fire burns large forest like the tongue controls the body
3:6	tongue is like a fire that burns the body
3:6	tongue stains the whole body
3:7–8	beasts can be tamed but the tongue is untamable
3:8	tongue is like restless evil
3:8	tongue is like deadly poison
3:9	tongue is like going to extremes
3:11	tongue not like a spring
3:12	tongue not like a fig tree
3:12	tongue compared to salt water
3:15	wisdom as earthly, unspiritual, devilish
3:17	heavenly wisdom is like fruit
3:18	peaceful people are like a farmer who harvests crop from seed
4:1–2	problems among Christians called wars
4:2	desires among Christians called murder
4:4	Christians compared to adulteresses
4:4	our relationship with God compared to friendship
4:7	our relationship with Satan compared to defensive move
4:8	our relationship with God compared to field maneuvers
4:8	our relationship with God compared to washing
4:9	our relationship with God compared to funeral
4:11–12	speaking evil compared to judging
4:13–14	faith compared to planning a trip
4:14	life like a mist
4:15	story of godly confidence
5:1–6	story of rich Christians
5:3	riches compared to a fire
5:5	riches compared to fat hearts
5:7	patient people are like farmers
5:9	Lord's closeness compared to standing at door
5:10	prophets' example of patience and suffering
5:11	Job's example of patience and suffering
5:14	scenario of sick person
5:17–18	Elijah's example of righteous prayer
5:19–20	spiritual weakness compared to being off course

Commands in the Book of James

1. Count it all joy
2. Let steadfastness have its full effect
3. Let him ask God
4. Let him ask in faith
5. That person must not suppose
6. Let the lowly brother boast

7. Let no one say
8. Do not be deceived
9. Know this
10. Be quick to hear
11. Be slow to speak
12. Be slow to anger
13. Put away
14. Be doers
15. Show no partiality
16. Listen
17. Speak
18. Act
19. Let not many become
20. Look at the ships
21. Do not boast
22. Do not be false to the truth
23. Submit to God
24. Resist the devil
25. Draw near to God
26. Clean your hands
27. Purify your hearts
28. Be wretched
29. Mourn
30. Weep
31. Let your laughter be turned to mourning
32. Humble yourselves
33. Do not speak evil against one another
34. Howl
35. Be patient
36. Establish your hearts
37. Do not grumble
38. Do not swear
39. Let him pray
40. Let him sing praises
41. Let him call
42. Let them pray
43. Confess sins
44. Pray for one another
45. Let him know

Does the book of James have a point? The "unstained from the world" line in James 1:27 suggests an investigation of how James uses the word "world." Later in the book, James takes one of his many illustrations to state a critical point about the "world": "Do you not know that friendship with the world is enmity with God? Therefore whoever wishes to be a friend of the world makes himself an enemy of God" (James 4:4).

Friendship with the world puts us into the "stained" position. Friendship with God keeps us in an "unstained" relationship. All those headed to church on Sunday morning want to be friends of God as much as we want to practice pure and undefiled religion. James uses friendship language to convey his point. If we become friends with the world's concerns, we create a gap between ourselves and God. If we seek friendship with God, we must create a gap between ourselves and worldly concerns.

James uses the word "world" in four places in his book. In James 4:4, he sets the world's concerns opposite God's. In James 3:6, he compares our tongue (that is, what we say) to a fire. When we speak the way the *world* speaks, our speech becomes a destructive fire. James already said in James 1:26 that religion involves the proper use of the tongue.

The other two uses of "world" occur in the "religion" passages in James 1:27–2:13. In the church assembly passage, James leaps from the economically poor ("a poor man in shabby clothing" in v. 2) to the *world* of the spiritually bankrupt ("has not God chosen those who are poor in the *world* to be rich in faith"), urging the people in Sunday morning church to welcome both those who have no money and those who have no faith. The fourth use comes in the description of "religion that is pure and undefiled," which is a religion in which the one seeking to be a friend of God "keeps oneself unstained from the *world*" (1:27).

James 4:4 thus offers a summary statement of the overall point of the book.[1] Nearly every paragraph in the five chapters relates to this message: James calls us to be friends with God. Friendship with God means creating distance between us and the impure, defiled (1:27), spiritually bankrupt (2:5), careless-in-speech world (3:6), and removing the gap between us and God by being the kind of person and doing the kinds of things God prizes in a friend. We embrace the values of God, not the ones the world holds. We don't think the way the world thinks; we think like God thinks.

---

[1] My summary relies on Luke Timothy Johnson, "Friendship with the World and Friendship with God: A Study of Discipleship in James," in *Brother of Jesus, Friend of God* (Grand Rapids: Eerdmans, 2004), 202–20.

Try reading the book of James through the lens of friendship. The sidebar provides one way of dividing James into smaller thought units and seeing each one through the eyes of friendship. In this reading, James 4:4 shows itself to be a summary of every paragraph in the book. Be friends with God!

> **"Do you not know that friendship with the world is enmity with God? Therefore whoever wishes to be a friend of the world makes himself an enemy of God" (James 4:4).**
>
> | | |
> |---|---|
> | 1:2–4 | testing a friendship makes it stronger |
> | 1:5–11 | a double-minded person is not a good friend |
> | 1:16–18 | friends of God know he provides |
> | 1:19–27 | friends of God "do" his bidding |
> | 2:1–13 | friends of God would not reject the poor from church |
> | 2:14–26 | real friendship means doing |
> | 3:1–12ff | friends know a cursing tongue cannot praise God |
> | 3:13–4:12 | envy is hostile to God and destroys friendship |
> | 4:13–16 | illustrations of people who forget God is in charge and ruin the friendship |
> | 5:1–6 | picture of friends of the world |
> | 5:7–20 | friendship demands patience, honesty, relationships, shepherding |

James makes it clear how the friends of God act: They love their neighbor as themselves (James 2:8). The neighbor includes the "orphans and the widows in their affliction" (1:27), the "poor man in shabby clothing" who comes into the assembly (2:2), and the "brother or sister" who is "ill-clad and in lack of daily food" (2:15). Being a friend of God includes "visiting" them (1:27), paying "attention" to them (2:3), and "giving them the things needed for the body" (2:16).

James's most pointed expression of being a friend with God comes in James 5:1–5. He offers two critiques. First, he points to those who have accumulated so many things that "your riches have rotted and your garments are moth-eaten" (5:2). James knows about the contents of their self-storage units and the extent of their bedroom closets. Second, he states that their wealth came at the expense of the poor (5:4–5). He links their wealth with the "affliction" of orphans and widows (1:27) and the "man in shabby clothing" in the Sunday assembly (2:2). James makes it clear that such people cannot be friends of God, for their abuse of the vulnerable "will be evidence against you and will eat your flesh like fire" (5:3). James imagines that God takes great offense at those who oppress the vulnerable.

So how does God's friend act? What does he do on the way to church? God's friends seek a pure, undefiled religion, take care of widows and orphans, keep unspotted from the world, welcome the economically poor into the pew, and reach out to those with a bankrupt faith. James 1:27 describes a friend of God. That's how James 1:27 fits in the book of James.

James 1:27 and the Bible

The book of James comes near the end of Scripture. At this point, most assume that all the core spiritual issues have been discussed earlier. Yet James 1:27 speaks of "pure religion." He raises unique issues, since no other verses in the New Testament talk about pure religion or orphans. Why does James, so late in the biblical story, make such a strong statement about the nature of "pure and undefiled religion?" How does this line fit within the broader spectrum of Scripture?

Not only does the book of James have a message, but the Bible itself contains a message. Articulating that entire message of the Bible is not the point of this short piece. On several occasions, Jesus addressed the issue of the central concerns of the Bible and God. He pointed to the two great commandments: love God (Deut. 6:5) and love others (Lev. 19:18). James takes up the former by describing what it means to be a friend of God. James 2:8 actually quotes the second great commandment. Who is the God believers should love with all their heart, soul, and might? Moses responds:

> For the LORD your God is God of gods and Lord of lords, the
> great, the mighty, and the terrible God, who is not partial and
> takes no bribe. (Deut. 10:17)

We recognize those lines from Sunday morning church! The "mighty . . . God" becomes the language of our hymns. Everything in heaven and earth belongs to him (Deut. 10:14). We sing of the God of gods and the Lord of lords. But Moses has more to say about this God who attracts all our love and worship. In the same breath he says,

> He executes justice for the fatherless and the widow, and loves
> the sojourner, giving him food and clothing. (Deut. 10:18)

The "Lord of lords" cares about orphans. The "God of gods" knows about widows. The "great, the mighty" keeps an eye on the sojourner.

Deuteronomy expands on the first great commandment with two principles: (1) you can't love the God you can't see if you don't love the people you do see, and (2) God evaluates the human community by how it treats its weakest members. Moses will explain the details throughout Deuteronomy, as the following explains.

Deuteronomy's Concern for the Vulnerable

Rest for the most vulnerable in the community (5:12–15)

Tithes to the weakest: orphans and widows (14:29)

Take care of the poor (15:7)

Economic guidelines on how the rich treat the poor (15:9)

Treatment of those in bondage (15:1–18)

Provide seats at the Passover for the orphans and widows (16:11)

Set up courts to protect the orphans and widows (24:17)

As Moses prepared Israel for setting up life in the Promised Land, he laid out how God would structure an ideal human community. But these principles do not end in Deuteronomy. At key points in the Bible story, these ideas resurface. Joshua emerged as a good leader because he maintained the standards of Deuteronomy. The judges fell below that standard. Every king in Judah and Israel received an evaluation based on how they measured up to Deuteronomy. Then look at these examples:

- 8th century BC—Isaiah lashes out at the people in Jerusalem. Why does Isaiah offer this critique? Isaiah says, "You are ignoring the poor, the widows, and the orphans." (See Isa. 1.)
- 7th century BC—Jeremiah critiques the people of Judah. Why is Jeremiah so negative? Jeremiah says, "You are ignoring the widows and orphans." (See Jer. 5 and 7.)

- 6th century BC—Ezekiel accuses the people of Jerusalem of wrongdoing. We wonder what they did wrong. "You mistreat the poor, the orphans, and the widows." (See Ezek. 22.)
- 5th century BC—Leaders ask Zechariah to weigh in on the issues involved in some worship wars. Zechariah lashes out. "Worship? You are mistreating the poor, the widows, and the orphans." (See Zech. 7.)
- 1st century AD—The apostles try to keep the children away from Jesus. The Lord becomes angry. Why are you angry, Jesus? Jesus says of the children, "For to such belongs the kingdom of God." (See Mark 10:13–16.)
- 1st century AD—The early church defies the local culture. What was the early church like? "There was not a needy person among them." (See Acts 2:45; 4:34.)
- 1st century AD—Church leaders gathered to deal with a problem. After the decision, they all agree. What about you, Paul? He said, "They would have us remember the poor, which very thing I was eager to do." (See Gal. 2:10.)
- 1st century AD—Paul writes the longest section of the Bible on giving. Why did you do that, Paul? In short, Paul says, "Your abundance at the present time should supply their want." (See 2 Cor. 8 and 9.)

So finally, we come to the end of the Bible, to one of the closing books of the New Testament. James writes that pure religion means taking care of the widows and orphans and welcoming the poor into your worship assembly.

We might ask James, "James, why did you say that? Where did you get that?"

He would say, "I read it in the Bible."

What does a friend of God do? God's friends take care of the vulnerable. Read Deuteronomy or the prophets or Psalms or Proverbs or Jesus or the early church. John put it this way: "He who does not love his brother whom he has seen, cannot love God whom he has not seen" (1 John 4:20).

Religion and Orphans and Widows

Those who seek friendship with God care about God's concerns. That's the point of James. God cares for the vulnerable. We can't love the God we cannot see if we don't love the people we do see, even if they come in shabby clothes to worship. Those who worship God are those who share his concerns. That's pure religion.

The fundamental issue at work lies in this question: Are ethics related to worship?

The prophets thought so. The passages in the box below offer a critique not of *the way* the people worshipped but because they sought to *worship without caring* for the vulnerable around them. The failure to see the connection between ethics and worship cost King Saul his throne (see 1 Sam. 15:22–23) and concerned King Jesus in his opening address to the world (see Matt. 5:23–24).

> What to me is the multitude of your sacrifices?
>   says the LORD;
> I have had enough of burnt offerings of rams
>   and the fat of fed beasts;
> I do not delight in the blood of bulls,
>   or of lambs, or of he-goats. . . .
>
> Bring no more vain offerings. . . .
>
> When you spread forth your hands,
>   I will hide my eyes from you;
> even though you make many prayers,
>   I will not listen;
>   your hands are full of blood.
> Wash yourselves; make yourselves clean;
>   remove the evil of your doings
>   from before my eyes;
> cease to do evil,
>   learn to do good;
> seek justice,
>   correct oppression;
> defend the fatherless,
>   plead for the widow. (Isa. 1:11, 13, 15–17)
>
> I hate, I despise your feasts,
>   and I take no delight in your solemn assemblies. . . .
>
> But let justice roll down like waters,
>   and righteousness like an ever-flowing stream. (Amos 5:21, 24)

Even the words betray a connection. The Hebrew and Greek words for "serve" go in the same two directions as the English word. *Serve* in English can mean a *worship service* or *service* at the soup kitchen.

The road to Sunday morning church goes through the book of James. James shows us how to be friends with God, how to care about what God cares about, and how to worship God with pure religion. After all, James would say, "I read it in the Bible."

WHAT DO YOU THINK?

1. What did James mean by "pure religion"? If you took a survey of your congregation, asking people if they practice "pure religion," what would they say? What would James say about the same group?

2. The chapter cites several biblical passages calling for God's people to take care of vulnerable children such as orphans. What do you think of these passages? Which resonated the most with you?

3. Discuss whether James was bringing up a new issue when he defined pure religion as caring for widows and orphans.

4. Why does this book deal more with orphans than with widows?

5. Do you practice pure religion?

6. Does your church practice pure religion?

PART 5

HOPE

Life is like a game of lost and found. One of the oft-lost items is hope. At crucial moments, we lose track of hope. As a result, we fall into despair or discouragement or just give up. If we decide to listen and make room, our ability to preserve depends on finding that lost hope. It gets hidden in different places. We find it in the most unusual spots; but without it, we often lose interest in listening and lose faith in making room.

36

LOST IN THE CITY

LUKE 2:41-52

AT&T aired a television commercial at Christmastime in 1996 that featured a teenage boy in what looked like downtown Chicago. Through the beams of the "L" platform, he saw a middle-aged woman on a corner. She sang the old hymn: "Amazing grace, how sweet the sound, that saved a wretch like me."

The boy seemed tired and bewildered. He wandered into a local café and ordered a drink at the counter. It quickly became apparent to the waiter that the boy was lost, likely a runaway, and when it came time to pay the bill, the man at the counter said, "No charge."

The boy walked the streets alone. He saw the same singing woman. "I once was lost, but now I'm found; was blind, but now I see."

The song jolted him into a decision. He found a phone booth, dialed, and the operator answered. He told her he needed to talk to his mother, but he didn't have any money. The operator quickly realized she was dealing with a runaway. She assured him that she'd put the call through.

In the next scene, the mother waited by the phone in a suburban kitchen. The phone rang. She answered. Silence. The boy spoke, "Mom." The mother responded, "Jimmy, is that you?"

It ended with a Greyhound bus pulling into the station. Jimmy got off and hugged his mother. The voice-over said, "We're ready. The call is free."

It's a familiar story. A boy is far away from home. He depends on the generosity of strangers. He comes to his senses and starts home. A single parent waits to greet him. The words hang in the background, "I once was lost, but now I'm found."

I don't know if AT&T still allows runaways to call free or if they train their staff to listen for the voice of a lost child, but the isolation and lostness is still there. Sociologists and urbanists often describe contemporary society with the word "isolation." We are separated from family, friends, and other people. Surrounded by people, we're lost and alone. We're lost because we lack direction, community, and hope.

Another young boy, like the one in the commercial, got lost in the big city. His parents searched for him frantically for three days. Finally, Mary and Joseph found their son Jesus. Perhaps out of that experience Jesus told stories about other people who were lost. The Gospel writer Luke filled his book with stories of sick people, broken men, outsiders, isolated women, and lost people. It may be one of the most relevant books of our time.

Jesus dealt with the lost in two ways.

First, he called them to community. He took a motley group of men and called them to be apostles. A fragmented group of women and men became his disciples. He healed lepers and welcomed them back into village life. He cured the sick and took them home to their families. He taught people about life and then served them a meal. He urged people to eat together, and not to exclude the isolated ones.

Something about community strikes at the core of being human. Jesus calls us to overcome our differences and form community. Isolation and real community are opposites.

Second, Jesus called people to God. When Jesus met the rejected outsiders, he offered them a place in God's kingdom. He urged women cast out by their peers to depend on the friendship of God. Jesus told the poor, who were isolated from the rest of the world, to seek the Lord. His message to each one was that with God, nobody is an outsider. You can't be so far from home that God can't find you. You can't be so lost in the city that God can't bring you home. You can't be so sick, so left out, or so rejected that God can't accept you. You can't be so ugly that God will turn away.

Jesus said life is like a father with two sons. The younger son asked for his share of the family inheritance. He took it and left home. The father hated to see him go, and he waited by the gate every day. The father wanted his son to come home more than anything else.

The son's life changed radically. He found new friends, friends who wanted to have a good time. He found new things to do, new places to see, new jobs to work, new crises to navigate, new tragedies to endure, and new sorrows to suffer.

The son finally realized that despite all that he had found, he was actually lost. He was lost from the security of a home, lost from family mealtime, lost from his comfortable bed, lost from fulfilling work, lost from prosperity, lost from relationships, and lost from his father.

So the son made a decision based on what he knew about his father. He realized that even a reluctant welcome home from his family would be superior to the depths to which he had traveled. He decided to go home. He prepared a strategy. He crafted his speech.

Meanwhile, the father still waited at the gate. He saw the boy at a distance and ran to meet him. He gave gifts. He offered the house keys. He threw a welcome party.

John Newton knew that story. He knew personally about being lost. So he wrote a song. "Amazing grace, how sweet the sound, that saved a wretch like me. I once was lost, but now I'm found; was blind, but now I see."

It's still a tough world out there. Hosts of people feel rejected. They live like pigs. They live temporarily far from home. They lose their family. They lose their friends. They no longer know the way or have any comfort. Fulfillment and integrity are forgotten values. They lack peace and purpose.

The father still waits at the gate. He still runs to meet you. He still gives gifts. He still passes on the house keys. He still throws a welcome party.

If you are lost and need to come home, remember that the call is free.

Continuities. I keep returning to the Luke 15 story about a father waiting at the gate, willing to listen and make room for his lost son. It's a perfect story. I suspect I also keep returning to this story because in it I find hope and a reason to go on.

WHAT DO YOU THINK?

1. Share a time of personal loneliness.

2. Name the various communities where you find companionship and acceptance.

3. Reflect on what it must be like not to have a community.

4. Does turning to God replace the need for community?

5. Have you ever been lost, either physically or spiritually? Share your story.

37

WE'VE COME
TO THE RIVER

ISAIAH 43:2

In 1996, a weekly news magazine ran a story with the title "A Bridge to Nowhere" about the challenges facing children in urban America.[1] It chronicled the poor conditions of the schools, the rampant crime, the widespread family unemployment, and the substandard housing. It said the children growing up there might as well be on a bridge that ended halfway across the river. For many of the children, the future seemed to be a dead end.

When I revisited that article twenty years later, it struck me how little had changed. America simply refuses to complete that bridge.

Marian Wright Edelman tells of one of those children, named Tony. He came to her attention through a private aid program in Washington, DC. The people who were giving out sandwiches and offering tutoring for boys like Tony asked him what he wanted for his twelfth birthday. He said, "What I want more than anything else is a bike. I've never had one."

Somebody had donated several used bikes to the center. They promised he would get his bike on his birthday. When he came to the center at age twelve, he changed his order. "I want a bag of groceries for my mother." They filled two bags and put a lemon meringue pie on the top. A volunteer offered to drive Tony home. The bags were too much for one boy to carry.

---

[1] David Gergen, "A Bridge to Nowhere" (editorial), *U.S. News & World Report*, September 9, 1996.

When they got to his house, the volunteer dropped one of the bags. Broken glass, food, bits of lemon meringue scattered over the ground. The volunteer and Tony both started to cry. Tony looked at the spoiled food and said, "That's the story of my life."

Tony is on a bridge to nowhere.

Our world is filled with despair. The despair comes because of poor schools, inequitable housing, low-paying jobs, terminal disease, broken glass, and spilled food.

Where do we turn in a world that writes editorials entitled "A Bridge to Nowhere"?

The prophet Isaiah knew about the world of despair, and perhaps he had those bridges to nowhere in mind when he wrote this line:

> When you pass through the waters I will be with you;
>> and through the rivers, they shall not overwhelm you;
> when you walk through the fire you shall not be burned,
>> and the flame shall not consume you. (Isa. 43:2)

Isaiah addressed people on a bridge to nowhere. They lived in Babylonian captivity. They imagined they would drown in the rivers of Babylon or be consumed by the fires of foreign domination. Far from home, they thought they would never again walk familiar streets or visit their favorite places. Nothing was left of what they wanted in life but broken glass and spilled food.

Isaiah told the people that at just the moment when you think you are on a bridge to nowhere, up steps the bridge-building God. Just when you think you might drown in your sorrows, the bridge-building God appears. Just when you think the river is too deep and the crossing is too wide, the bridge-building God makes a way.

Isaiah repeatedly returns to images similar to a bridge-building God.

- When the road ahead is crooked, God straightens it out (Isa. 40:3).
- When chasms block the way, God fills them in (Isa. 40:4).
- When the ocean has to be crossed, God cuts a path through the middle (Isa. 43:16).
- When the desert keeps us from our destination, God builds a road (Isa. 43:19).

- When a fire rages, God provides a protective shield (Isa. 43:2).
- When the river is wide, God builds a bridge (Isa. 43:2).

God has always done that. He takes on situations where there seems to be no solution. He saves people who have no redeeming value. He restores neighborhoods of people bent on evil. He revives nations that don't seem worth preserving. He saves a world bent on war. He redeems those who murder, cheat, and abuse others. In each case, he leads them through the rivers and guides them through the fire.

God loves to build bridges: seeing bridges for the blind, hearing bridges for the deaf, freedom bridges for the enslaved, serving bridges for those in despair, helping bridges for those standing in the middle of broken glass and spilled food.

God does his best work for people on bridges to nowhere. No river is too wide for God. No water is too deep for God. No fire is too hot for God. No flame is too high for God.

He loves to deliver his people. He loves to call the down-and-out and lift them up. He loves to reach out to those on the outside and bring them in. He loves to lift up the weary and faint and make them mount up with wings like eagles. He loves to speak to people knee-deep in work, up to their elbows in problems, and show them how to finish the bridge to nowhere.

When we lived in Memphis, we learned about a group of women on a bridge to nowhere. Every night, hundreds of women found themselves pregnant, unwed, and homeless. A series of poor decisions, bad breaks, soured relationships, societal barriers, and dead-end roads led them to their predicament. Working through Agape Child and Family Services, we began Families in Transition. We provided housing, furniture, medical care during the delivery of their baby, counseling, Bible study, life skills training. For thirty months, we surrounded them with compassion and security and help. We started that program in 2005, and now, over fourteen years later, we have helped more than five hundred women. Not a single one, not one, has slipped back onto that road to nowhere. God builds bridges.

What keeps God from working through us to build more bridges? Isaiah addresses that issue in Isaiah 42:18: God's own people become blind and deaf. We can't be the light if we haven't seen the light. God knew that people who should be able to see would close their eyes, that people who should be able to hear would turn a deaf ear. God knew those people who could make room would close their doors. Those charged with bringing light would sit in darkness.

We've come to the river. Do we sit by the shore and argue among ourselves or do we join God in making a way across the water?

The earliest and most sustained efforts of Churches of Christ to help those in despair may be the agencies that serve children. Taking care of at-risk children is not a backdoor ministry of God's people. It is the practice of pure religion. Caring for vulnerable children like Tony is the front door of the church. It's not something we do if we have the money; it's central to the mission of the church.

Vulnerable children, orphaned or unwanted in some way, exist around the world. Some seventeen thousand children will die today around the world because they lack food, clean water, or existing medicines for curable diseases. While you've been reading this chapter, several children in America have died from violence or neglect. Children everywhere are on a bridge to nowhere. We serve a God who builds bridges.

If congregations were to join God in this task, if Churches of Christ took the lead to save the unwanted children of America, if Christians around the world joined hands with the God standing at the edge of the river, then the world would want to know about Churches of Christ. You would have to reopen the balcony, double up every service, because people would want to know what you believe and who enabled you to build that bridge.

We have come to the river. What will we do?

Continuities. All of us sometimes feel like we are on a bridge to nowhere. Those who have no voice and own no room see the bridge to nowhere as a trap from which they cannot escape. Those of us who seek to hear and make room often join them on that bridge. Hope comes when we realize that God builds all bridges.

WHAT DO YOU THINK?

1. If we take time to listen, we will hear stories of people on a bridge to nowhere. Share stories you have heard.

2. Isaiah mentions promises God made to vulnerable people. Do we believe those promises?

3. List some ways God's promises would enable you to listen to vulnerable people.

4. List some ways you and others could make room.

5. Does your congregation have ministries that build bridges? What are they? If not, begin to pray that your church can listen and join God in building bridges.

38

LET THE PAST
BE THE PAST—AT LAST

1 JOHN 1:5-10

Jeffrey Abrams did the screenplay for a movie called *Regarding Henry* in 1991. It followed the life of a successful New York City attorney named Henry who cheats, connives, ignores his family, and runs over other people. He shows no awareness of his brutal and abusive behavior. Then one night when he stops at a convenience store, he finds himself in the middle of a robbery and gets shot in the head.

With severe brain damage, he begins a long period of rehabilitation and in the process goes through a transformation of personality. He learns to walk again, talk again, and begins to communicate with his family and to care. In short, Henry becomes a good person.

One reviewer claimed the movie underlined the difficulty most people have in changing bad habits. She ended the review by asking, If we want to change, are the choices only magic or brain damage?

We all wonder the same thing. Can a person change? Can we remove the past? We all know some people who never seem to improve. We wonder about things in our own past that seem fixed in place. Does our past have to dictate our future? Are our only choices magic or brain damage?

John gives us another option in 1 John. He based his conclusion on his personal knowledge of Jesus Christ. John had seen him, touched him, heard him, and spent time with him. He knew Jesus, and he knew what Jesus could do. One thing Jesus could do was remove the past.

He said it this way:

> This is the message we have heard from him and proclaim to
> you, that God is light and in him is no darkness at all. If we say
> we have fellowship with him while we walk in darkness, we lie
> and do not live according to the truth; but if we walk in the
> light, as he is in the light, we have fellowship with one another,
> and the blood of Jesus his Son cleanses us from all sin. If we say
> we have no sin, we deceive ourselves, and the truth is not in us.
> If we confess our sins, he is faithful and just, and will forgive
> our sins and cleanse us from all unrighteousness. If we say we
> have not sinned, we make him a liar, and his word is not in us.
> (1 John 1:5–10)

John reminds us of those television commercials advertising some new improved cleaner that promises to take out the most stubborn stains on your carpet and make it look new again. Jesus is the perfect cleanser. He does not remove physical stains and dirt, but the guilt and stain of sin. This cleanser works on all blemishes, all stains. There is nothing in the past that this cleanser can't dissolve. It's new, improved, commercial strength, and more.

You can't name a sin Jesus can't remove. Let's say there are five thousand ways to sin. Let's say you are the worst sinner in the world and you have sinned in all five thousand ways. Then, you think of another five thousand ways to sin. When you come to Jesus, he removes all ten thousand sins.

Verse nine in the passage above tells us he cleanses us from all unrighteousness. Righteousness is a relationship word. Unrighteousness means we've lived in a way that ruined our past relationships. We may not be right with our spouse or neighbor or boss or brother or Jesus or God. It doesn't matter what kind of relationship you have messed up, Jesus can clean up that unrighteousness.

Perhaps you've seen the commercial with an adolescent boy playing soccer in his best clothes. He comes into the house and his white shirt is green. His mother takes the shirt, puts it in the water, and adds the featured laundry detergent, and the shirt comes out looking like it just came off the rack at the clothing store.

Commercials want us to be believers. We never see a commercial where the mother refuses to try the product, where she takes her son's shirt and throws it in the trash, or where she looks at the camera and says, "I don't think it works."

What about us? Do we believe these lines: "The blood of Jesus his Son cleanses us from all sin" and "he . . . will forgive our sins and cleanse us from all unrighteousness"?

When we appear before God, he will open the book of our life. We often fear what he might read or what he might say. He'll scan the entries, then say, "She walked in the light," or "He has no unrighteousness."

The book will have nothing about our fractured relationships or our anger or our adultery or our bitterness. Just, "She walked in the light. He was cleansed by the blood of Jesus. They are washed clean."

Jesus can undo what sin has done. My sin pushed me over the edge, but Jesus was there to catch me. My sin crushed me under its weight, but Jesus lifted off the heavy load. My sin broke my spirit, but Jesus gave it new life. His blood can restore the most discolored soul. His death washes the nastiest dirt away.

Ernest Hemingway wrote a short story called "The Capital of the World." In it, he referred to an incident about a boy named Paco. It began, "Madrid is full of boys named Paco." Then he told this story. A father and son had a falling-out. The son, angry and bitter, left for Madrid. The father cooled down and later followed his son to the city. He put an advertisement in the metropolitan paper. It said, "Paco, meet me at Hotel Montana, Noon, Tuesday. All is forgiven." The ad was signed "Papa."

That day, the authorities had to call out the Spanish National Guard. Eight hundred young men named Paco had gathered in front of the hotel.[1]

Hemingway writes a parable of our lives. We are the banished son. We stomped out in anger. Somewhere, we all have a papa we both love and hate. We see the ad in the paper. We rush to the hotel. We hope against hope that all is forgiven.

---

[1] Ernest Hemingway, "The Capital of the World," in *The Complete Short Stories of Ernest Hemingway* (New York: Scribner, 1987), 38.

But then Hemingway's parable breaks down. Eight hundred boys want forgiveness, but there's only one papa. At least seven hundred and ninety-nine are disappointed.

The gospel ends differently. We all rush to the hotel. We join the massive throng of all humanity. Then we look up. Towering over all our fears, our regrets, our apprehensions, and our pains is one figure. There in the midst of people so desperately wanting forgiveness from their father is the cross of Jesus Christ. What he did is enough for all humanity.

We wallow in the past. We play the video in our minds of what we did wrong. We feel the pain, the hurt again and again. We toss and tumble at night. We avoid that spot. We never say that name. We get stuck in that position. We did something, and we can't move on. We hurt somebody, and we relive it every day. We were part of something wicked, and we can't let go. We think it will take magic or brain surgery to fix what we've done.

I know it takes time to process all of this chaos. We don't heal our hurts overnight. God is not rushing you. But you need to know that Jesus is there saying without a doubt, "I can take care of that. I can take it away."

He tells us, "Be clean and live life."

Continuities. We feel that sin dominates our world. It affects us and keeps us from doing what we want to do. It affects the vulnerable of the world and makes us think there is no point in listening or making room. Look again. Jesus removes all sin.

WHAT DO YOU THINK?

1. Why do so many have difficulty accepting forgiveness?

2. Why do we continue to feel guilty even when we know we can be forgiven?

3. How does guilt keep us from listening and making room?

4. Does the Bible or Jesus put any conditions on forgiveness? What are they?

39

HOW CAN I FIND FAITH IN ALL THE TROUBLE I'VE HAD?

PSALM 22:1-8

Some time ago at the end of a sermon, a woman responded to the invitation. Facing a major problem in life, she sought our support and prayers. Several of her friends joined her as the church elders gathered around and we prayed. The elders promised to pray for her that week.

I remember thinking, "There's another problem solved." I put the issue out of my mind. Her friends would support her, and with the whole church praying, she could start with a clean slate.

A year later, I visited with that same woman. She still faced the same problem. Her friends hugged her, she got a few cards in the mail, elders stopped her in the hallway to give encouraging words, but all of them did what I did. They marked it "Problem solved."

I thought about her friends. They were the best kind—faithful, not superficial. They willingly walked with this sister. Several elders expressed deep concern. But none of us knew it was an unresolved problem.

Unresolved problems exist everywhere. We push them out of our mind. We say a kind word. We buy a gift. We meet them for coffee. And then we deny that the problem continues to exist. But the person knows the problem is not solved.

We know their names: Alcoholism. Alzheimer's. Cancer. Domestic abuse. Injustice. Inequity. Racism. Misery. Pain. All unsolved problems.

Our culture makes it worse. It convinces us that there is a pill, a treatment, a place, a car, or a diamond that overcomes all that life sends our way. But despite the proposed solutions, there are unsolved problems.

Our churches often make it worse. "Come to church and be happy." We wear our best smiles and have a positive mental attitude. We quote Paul telling us to "rejoice in the Lord always." But despite the proposed solutions, there are unsolved problems.

Jesus asked his father three times in the Garden of Gethsemane to solve a problem. We think, Now we're on to something. His friends prayed nearby. The garden offered solitude. But the police came, and he was arrested.

Then came a series of trials: first before the Sanhedrin, and then in front of Pilate. Jesus faced the angry mob, encountered the soldiers, met the executioner, and joined the thieves. Hanging on the cross, Jesus confronted an unsolvable problem. The trust of the garden seemed forgotten. The legion of angels did not come. Being at the right hand of God offered no present advantage. We're stunned at what he said, "My God, my God, why have you forsaken me?" (Matt. 27:46).

Did God give up on Jesus? Did he walk away as our church seemed to walk away from the woman who sought our help? Why did Jesus say those words?

Jesus quoted Psalm 22:1. Some think Jesus drew on those words as a source of comfort, but Psalm 22 offers little relief.

Think of the lines Jesus might have quoted:

- "The LORD is my shepherd, I shall not want" (Ps. 23:1).
- "The earth is the LORD's and the fullness thereof" (Ps. 24:1).
- "To thee, O LORD, I lift up my soul" (Ps. 25:1).

Instead, he quoted Psalm 22:1. What's happening at this moment on the cross? What did Jesus find here during an unsolvable problem? How can he be our Savior when he seemed not to believe?

Psalm 22 is a lament psalm. Of the one hundred and fifty psalms, some sixty-three are laments. We often ignore these psalms. We seldom read them in worship. We generally don't study them in class. We don't sing many of them in service. Few best-selling books talk about lament.

But life comes with lament. Lament psalms help. They work. They have power. They do two things.

First, the lament psalm admits there are seemingly unsolvable problems. In an upbeat culture that thinks about success, happiness, and optimism, and avoids what causes pain, hurt, and loss, the lament psalms say, "Some things are not right."

Psalm 22 tells us life is out of order. We face massive disorientation and anguish. It lists our troubles and then throws the list at God.

Psalm 22 reminds us that we can tell God anything. We can be angry with God. We can be in a rage against God. Whatever our condition, we can say, "God, what are you going to do about this?"

Complaining to God puts a finger on the trouble. I am in a crisis. I'm in a rage. Our problems come out of the darkness, and by voicing them to God, they come into the light.

Jesus complained to God about his troubles. God, did you watch the series of trials? God, do you feel the nails? God, do you hear the ridicule? "My God, my God, why have you forsaken me?"

Second, lament psalms give God control. Once God hears the anger, the rage, the confusion, the frustration, the lament prayer turns it over to God. "God, things are out of control on your planet. I'd like to take vengeance, but I'm turning it over to you. I'd like to give them a piece of my mind, but I'm letting you do the work."

There's a certain arrogance and pride that makes us think we can deal with all our issues. We come to believe we can conquer all diseases, stop all evil, correct all wrongs, or deal with all the bad. Then we run into those unsolvable problems. Lament psalms help us give them to God.

Jesus never requested the help of the angels. His anger and rage and pain may have wanted to, but he never put in the call. Jesus gave himself up to God on the cross.

The cross offered no easy out, but he prayed the lament. Even as the Son of God, he suffered, groaned, and died because he submitted to God.

In Gethsemane, Jesus prayed for deliverance from his fate. Then came the police, the trials, the crowd, the cross, the pain. On the cross, he let go and trusted God to carry him through.

We all face the seemingly unsolvable. Our faith offers us a seldom-used option: the lament psalms. There are sixty-three of them. The thirteen to start with are Psalms 6, 13, 22, 35, 38, 51, 79, 86, 88, 102, 130, 137, and 143. If life is really bad, worse than most people have to endure, add a fourteenth: Psalm 109.

In the movie *Sophie's Choice*, Stingo took a train traveling from Washington, DC, to New York City. Two close friends had committed suicide. He went to bury them. Stingo sat on the train crying. A woman sitting next to him knew Scripture. She gave him the best gift possible. She shared with him Psalm 88. As the train went through New Jersey, she worked her way through the complaint, to the giving up of control to God, to submission to his will.

Then she said, "That's one fine psalm."

We all face unsolvable problems, but we have been given a resource. Pray the lament psalms.

Continuities. Most of us tend to think we can solve most problems. As we listen to the vulnerable, we start to formulate a plan. As we move them into new space, we have a goal in mind. Then we hit a wall. What do we do when the problem is unsolvable? We do what Jesus did. We turn to the lament psalms.

WHAT DO YOU THINK?

1. Share a story about an unsolvable problem.

2. What kinds of seemingly insurmountable issues might be encountered in listening and making room?

3. How can the lament psalms reframe our listening and making room?

4. Why do we tend to ignore the lament psalms?

5. What problem are you facing? Write a lament psalm concerning the issue.

40

REFRESHMENT

LUKE 15:13-31

An inner-city minister and I visited a house off Crump Boulevard in Memphis where four sisters and two babies lived. The house was unpainted. The raw wood floor was covered with debris. The furniture was worn and dirty. Everything in the house was filthy.

It was not a nice place, and these were not nice people. One sister had just been released from jail for stabbing her boyfriend. The fourteen-year-old had AIDS. All four were promiscuous, used gutter language, and showed us little respect.

As we visited, I started watching the baby girl. Clad in only a diaper, she went from one sister to another seeking affection. They pushed her away. One slapped her and pushed her to the floor. She couldn't get any attention.

Then she sat down on the dirty floor and saw a cold piece of meat on the top of a pile of trash. She crawled over to the pile. She reached out her hand. She picked up the gob of meat and moved it toward her mouth.

That moment is etched in my mind. I wanted to jump up, pick her up, and rescue her. I wanted to take the dirty piece of meat out of her little hand. I wanted to give her some attention. I wanted to show her some love. I wanted to keep her away from that dirty food.

But I didn't. I just sat there. I never touched that baby. I never showed her any love. I'm not ashamed of what I did, but of what I didn't do.

I have this strange bone in my body. I call it my "I don't want to" bone. I don't want to pick up a dirty baby. I don't want to embrace a teenager with

AIDS. I don't want to shake hands with a homeless man. I don't want to wipe the nose of a sick child that doesn't belong to me. I don't want to sit on the cot next to a man serving a sentence for murder.

So what is a person like me to do? How do I get rid of my "I don't want to" bone? What will turn it into an "I want to" bone? How do I get off that chair and pick up that baby? How do I overcome my resistance? What will get me out of my comfort zone?

C. S. Lewis compared the issue to fuels.[1] What propels our lives? What fuel makes us do what we dream of doing?

Some try guilt. Guilt is a strong motivator. At times, it is quite appropriate. We know how guilt is done. We can recite the arguments: "You mean after God took you back into his arms, you can't pick up that little baby?" "After all Jesus did for you, you have never led a person to Christ? You can't go to heaven by yourself; you must take somebody with you." "How can you tell me there are hungry, dying children in your city and you've never helped?"

Guilt is a powerful fuel. But it gets terrible mileage. It doesn't last. It won't endure. We have to go to the guilt station too often to fill up for it to be an effective fuel.

Others try fear. Fear is also a powerful fuel. There is great truth behind fear. We've heard about fear all our lives. "What happens if that little baby gets food poisoning and dies?" "What if the Lord comes this weekend?" "If we don't rescue those children today, there may be no tomorrow." "You mean you didn't say anything? Don't you know you may never have an opening like that again?"

Fear certainly motivates, but it has little long-term effectiveness. It does not restore our soul. It doesn't refresh our spirit. It is not an efficient motivator. We have to refuel too often with fear to get anything long-term done.

Some try success. The fuel of success is quite powerful as well. At its core, there are profound truths about success. Many church consultants promote this fuel. We've heard the stories. "We started with three people meeting in a bar, and now we have three thousand on Sunday morning."

---

[1] C. S. Lewis, *Mere Christianity* (New York: Macmillan Publishing Company, 1977), 54.

"We baptized eighty-five last year using this method." All the lectureships want you to speak when you have a thirty-million-dollar building with your own freeway exit. "We served five thousand children with school supplies last year."

Success beckons us. We want to be like those who have soared. Their stories give us a goal, but not much gumption. They inspire us, but it doesn't last. We have to hear more stories every year to keep going. We travel back to the success station to get refueled.

What fuel can we use? What will change our "I don't want to" bone into a "want to" bone? What propels ministry? What makes us share our faith? What makes us help the poor? What makes us care for unwanted children?

In Luke 15, we hear sounds of joy. There's dancing, a band playing, a party going on. We hear music and shouting. In fact, the whole chapter is about parties. The people in this chapter get refreshed. The whole village celebrated when they found that lost sheep. The woman's friends came over to party when she located that lost coin. The father called for the fatted calf and the celebration because the son came home.

The parable of the prodigal son may be the greatest story in the Bible. It covers the range of emotions: hate, pleasure, anger, love, regret, dissatisfaction, longing, sensuality, joy, bitterness, loyalty, grief, sorrow, surprise, greed, and stubbornness. This one parable speaks of all the major biblical doctrines: grace, love, lostness, repentance, forgiveness, mission, God, guilt, and salvation.

But it also tells us what refreshes our lives and our work. The key to the parable comes in verse 20. The father waits at the door for the younger son. When he returns home, the father sees the boy, and we find out what fuels his life.

The father doesn't wait at the gate out of *guilt*. "I should never have let him go. I'm a bad father, and now I must make up for it. If I wait here long enough, enough times, and dedicate myself to fixing my mistake, maybe the guilt will go away."

That's not why the father waited at the gate.

Nor does he wait for the younger son out of *fear*. "If I'm not here when he comes, he may pass by. He may lose his nerve when he gets close to home. I better check out every traveler, answer every call. Maybe if I wait here every day, some other wanderer will tell him, and he'll come home."

That's not why the father waited at the gate.

The father was not motivated by *success*. "I want the boy back so people will see that I'm a good father. We will set an example for how a good family deals with conflict and tragedy. The neighbors did that with their daughter. Her father waited at the gate for her, and she came home and now they have the approval of all."

That's not why the father waited at the gate.

It says he was filled with compassion.

The father in the story represents God. Jesus tells us what the rest of the Bible confirms. **The fuel that empowers God is compassion.** It comes with many names: love, *agape* (the Greek word for love), mercy, *hesed* (the Hebrew word for loving kindness), compassion. They all describe the fuel that drives God toward us.

It's compassion that made him walk in the garden, put the rainbow in the sky, stand with Abraham, send Moses to free the slaves, choose David, dispatch the prophets, and send his Son. For God so loved the world that he gave us his Son.

Compassion is the fuel that drives the story. Compassion keeps the father waiting on the wayward son. Compassion draws the prodigal home. Compassion sends the father to the field to talk to the older brother. Compassion makes it the perfect story.

Compassion is the self-renewing fuel. Guilt runs out, and we have to find a guilt station to refuel. Fear wears us out, and we have to get repairs. Success is so transient that it's gone before we can celebrate. But compassion lasts, renews, refreshes, restores, rebuilds, rebounds, and revives.

Compassion draws us to God and God to us. It leads us to reach out to others, even those we find repulsive. Compassion drives us just as it moved the father. Compassion makes us all we ever wanted to be. It makes this story the perfect story of life.

Continuities. We often listen and make room out of guilt, fear, or as a desire for success. None of that works very long. As we listen to the vulnerable child, we need to listen to our own hearts to see what drives us. As we make room, we need to make sure there is room in our soul for compassion.

WHAT DO YOU THINK?

1. Give an example of helping others out of guilt.

2. Give an example of helping others out of fear.

3. Give an example of helping others in order to look successful.

4. Are there other fuels besides the three the author names that cause people to help others?

5. List some practical ways to keep compassion as our fuel.

6. The New Testament often refers to the compassion of Jesus. How and why did he show compassion?

41

RUN WITH
THE HORSES

JEREMIAH 12:1-6

Stephen Covey, in his book *The Seven Habits of Highly Effective People,* tells about finding a man cutting down a tree in the forest. Covey asked, "What are you doing?" The man responded with some anger. "Can't you see, I'm sawing down this tree?" Covey observed, "You look exhausted. How long have you been at it?" The man replied, "Five hours. I'm beat. This work is hard." Covey proposed, "Why don't you take a break for a few minutes and sharpen your saw. I'm sure the work would go faster." The man answered quickly, "I don't have time to sharpen the saw. I'm too busy sawing."[1]

We all have reasons for being tired. Maybe it's too much physical labor. It could be the long hours. For some, there are just too many tasks. Others get tired from the boredom. Perhaps we grow weary trying to move things that can't be moved.

Covey made a good point with his story. We saw, but never sharpen. We live, but never know why. We exist, but never triumph. We wear down, but never get restored.

The title and inspiration for this chapter come from Eugene Peterson's *Run with the Horses* (Downers Grove: InterVarsity Press, 1983).
[1]Stephen R. Covey, *The Seven Habits of Highly Effective People* (New York: Simon & Schuster, 1989), 287.

Exhaustion is not just a modern trait. Weary people filled the ancient world. People who cut, but never sharpened. People who lived, but never knew why.

But in the middle of the ancient world came a group of people who told another story. They were tired, but never worn out. They were weary, but not exhausted. They were beaten, but not defeated. We call them the prophets. We hear their voices from almost three thousand years ago. They were men who wrote from the bottom of wells and in the midst of battle. They challenged their world to look in a different direction.

Jeremiah was one of those weary prophets. One day, a group of young men gathered on a street corner in Anathoth. They didn't like what Jeremiah had been preaching. One of them spoke in a riddle, "Let's chop down the tree while it's still healthy." They laid plans to kill Jeremiah.

Jeremiah didn't understand. He pleaded with God. "I've put myself into your hands. I proclaimed your message. How in the world can bad men win over good men? How can I live when so many are against me? How do people keep going when nothing goes right?"

God gave him a strange answer: "If you have raced with men on foot, and they have wearied you, how will you compete with horses? And if in a safe land you fall down, how will you do in the jungle of the Jordan?" (Jer. 12:5).

What does that mean? We all get tired racing against other people. Who can win a race with a horse? It's exhausting living in urban America. Who could survive the jungle?

God's point was that Jeremiah didn't run alone. He drew on another source of support. And Jeremiah not only survived the boys from Anathoth, he thrived. He didn't live an average life, he soared.

Isaiah was another prophet faced with the same situation. People all around him seemed discouraged and defeated. When they tried to walk, they fell down. When they tried to run, they grew weak. Even the young men and women in his time grew tired and dejected.

Isaiah walked into the middle of the crowd. "This isn't right! Have you people not heard? Did you not know? Where have you been? Have you forgotten?" Then Isaiah gives one of the clearest explanations of God found anywhere:

> The LORD is the everlasting God, the Creator of the ends of the earth. He does not faint or grow weary, his understanding is unsearchable. He gives power to the faint, and to him who has no might he increases strength. Even youths shall faint and be weary, and young men shall fall exhausted; but they who wait for the LORD shall renew their strength, they shall mount up with wings like eagles, they shall run and not be weary, they shall walk and not faint. (Isa. 40:28–31)

He never tires. He never falls down exhausted. He is inexhaustible. And he shares that strength with those who follow him.

The way to soar in life is to root our existence in God. He can lift you so high above your problems you will fly like an eagle. You'll see things from a different perspective. From those lofty heights, everything takes on a different color, a brighter hue, a newer shine. You will see what you never saw before. You will connect to a source of energy you've never known before.

The prophets knew that our energy came from our sense of self. If who we are is defined by society, we will have no more energy than society. If our self is defined by family, our energy will never rise above family. If we root our identity in education, we must rely on that education for our energy.

But if our sense of being comes from God, then our energy is boundless because he is boundless. We'll find our stamina enduring because his stamina endures. Our vitality will be perpetual because he is perpetual.

If we build life around another person, we will never rise above that person. If we idolize and imitate a star, we will be tied to their humanness. If the best we ever strive for is a beloved teacher, we will never rise above that teacher. We are doomed to crash just as all those people will crash.

If our definitions of reality don't make it beyond the bedroom, if our view of the world comes through our wallet, if we build our life around being different from the people we don't like, our vision of tomorrow will repeat the worst of today.

But if God is the source of our energy, if that's what captures our mind, then we'll run with the horses and soar with the eagles. We'll see life through a different lens. We'll see peace in the midst of war, solutions in the face of problems, new life when we're surrounded by decay, and home in the midst of being a refugee.

One day in Memphis, I spent the afternoon with a man I'll call Melvin. As we talked, we heard a gunshot outside his apartment. He knew all about this neighborhood. It's where he killed a man. He shot him in cold blood. They sent him to prison. In the confines of prison, he found freedom in God. Now you should hear Melvin talk. Despite all the mistakes he's made, beyond all the hardship he brought on his family, even with the horrible memories of prison, life is new. He's running with the horses. He's flying like an eagle.

Continuities. Most of the literature from the ancient world is either gone or in the back room of a museum. But the writings of the prophets, including Isaiah and Jeremiah, continue to be read and regularly inspire the readers. Those who listen to the vulnerable do well to listen to the prophets. Those who seek to make room can draw their plans from men like Isaiah and Jeremiah.

WHAT DO YOU THINK?

1. The chapter centers on Jeremiah 12 and Isaiah 40. Which passage is most meaningful to you?

2. Give examples of how we seek to imitate our favorite star or teacher. Discuss the implications of that imitation.

3. Believing in God's power to frame our existence is part of our worldview. What worldviews do you hear on a regular basis? What is the Christian worldview?

4. Consider memorizing the passages from Jeremiah 12 and Isaiah 40 so that they are readily available.

5. What do you know about eagles? Why do you think an eagle is used in the verses talking about God and renewal?

42

HOW TO FINISH
THE RACE

2 TIMOTHY 2:1-8

As a young minister, I worked with another preacher whom I'll call Mike. He had excellent skills, people loved him, and he taught the Bible well. We served on the same church staff for a short time, and then I moved. Mike and his wife came to visit us later when we lived in Milwaukee. They stayed at our house, took us to an expensive German restaurant, sat in our living room, and offered us memorable words of encouragement. I felt mentored, guided, and uplifted, and when Mike left, I was ready to stay in ministry forever.

A couple of weeks later, I learned that Mike left his position on the church staff. Confused and perplexed, I investigated and found out Mike had another woman. A woman in the congregation he served came for counseling; they ignored the proper safeguards and got romantically involved. Just after he visited us, the affair became public. Mike was out.

I felt angry and betrayed. Mike ate at my table, slept in my house, stayed with my family, encouraged me in ministry, and pointed me to Scripture, but during all that time, he was deep in sin. He pretended to be happily married while at my house but was living another life back home.

I've never been able to get Mike out of my mind. He started the race strong, preached for a large church, rose to be a godly leader, reached back to help young families like mine, then stumbled, fell, and quit the race.

He's not alone. Israel picked twelve leaders to spy out the Promised Land. Ten came back defeated. They urged the people to drop out of the race. Three great kings led the united kingdom in ancient Israel: Saul, David, and Solomon. They all started the race with high hopes, but all three stumbled and fell. Jesus chose twelve apostles, men mentored by the Son of God. Judas started with that group, but he faltered and never finished the race. In 2 Timothy, we see the names of twenty-four Christians, people who worked side by side with the apostle Paul. Twenty-four started the race; six toppled and fell.

In his book *Finishing Strong*, Steve Farrar tells of John Bisagno, the long-term preacher at a megachurch in Houston. As a young preacher fresh out of school, John bought a new Bible. Inside the cover, he wrote the names of the twenty-four men who completed school with him. Each had a burning desire to serve God all their lives. He listed two dozen preachers out to change the world. Bisagno kept up with the men on the list and occasionally crossed off the name of a man who stumbled and quit. When Bisagno turned 53, only three names remained on the list. Twenty-one started, but did not finish.[1]

We all know friends we had in high school. We watched them commit their lives to Jesus. We witnessed their baptism into Christ. Statistics say about one-third drop out before they finish their teen years.

This issue is taken up in depth in 2 Timothy. Paul writes to Timothy urging him to remain faithful, to stay the course, to finish strong. Don't quit. Don't give up. Don't stumble. The athletic metaphor comes up near the end.

> As for you, always be steady, endure suffering, do the work of an evangelist, fulfil your ministry. For I am already on the point of being sacrificed; the time of my departure has come. I have fought the good fight, I have finished the race, I have kept the faith. Henceforth there is laid up for me the crown of righteousness, which the Lord, the righteous judge, will award to me on that Day, and not only to me but also to all who have loved his appearing. (2 Tim. 4:5–8)

---

[1] Steve Farrar, *Finishing Strong: Going the Distance for Your Family* (Sisters, OR: Multnomah, 2000), 15–16.

The "good fight" is not a military image, but a boxing match or a foot race. "Finished the race" means he didn't drop out, but crossed the finish line. The "crown" refers not to a king, but the victor's wreath. He got the trophy, the winner's flag, or the gold.

Paul reflected on thirty years of ministry, on the shipwrecks, persecution, and disappointment. He knew about his imprisonment and likely execution. He concluded: I have finished the race.

He challenged Timothy: Don't give in to lust (2:22). Don't become greedy or prideful or turn to worldly living (3:2–4). Don't leave the core Christian beliefs (4:3–4). Maintain the discipline of the athlete. Obey like a well-trained soldier. Work diligently like a farmer. Beyond the race is the reward, the victory, the prize.

All this raises questions. What keeps us from quitting? What made Paul finish the race? How can we be like Caleb and Joshua and not the other ten spies? What makes us like Hezekiah and Josiah, not Saul and Solomon? How can we be like John, not Judas? Like Timothy, not Demas? Two lines stand out in the book.

The first line is this one: "Be strong in the grace that is in Christ Jesus" (2:1). Finishing the race has everything to do with grace. The message is not to be strong yourself, but to be strong in grace.

You have read the stories about Winston Churchill's ability to never give up despite repeated rejection. Alexander Graham Bell never quit, even though nobody backed his early telephones. Yogi Berra never stopped, even when he couldn't hit or throw. Wilma Rudolph overcame polio to win three gold medals in the Olympics.

The stories inspire me, but they also threaten me. What if I don't have that kind of stamina? What if I don't have the strength to pull myself up by my own bootstraps? What if I am not naturally resilient? Do I drop out of the race because I didn't have it in me in the first place?

Be strong in the grace that is in Christ Jesus. I am not alone. It's not a matter of gusty persistence; it's a matter of being strong in God's mercy. God's grace gives me reason to do right, reason to run, reason to reach the grace goal.

The second line is "Remember Jesus Christ" (2:8). Finishing the race has everything to do with Jesus. If we forget Jesus, there's no way to finish strong. If we remember Jesus, there's not much way to fail.

When we take our eyes off Jesus, worship turns cold, goals get fuzzy, our mind gets cluttered, ministry gets lost, persecutions seem eternal, and we start looking somewhere else to get power to finish the race.

Hardships will come. We will face our own versions of shipwrecks, prisons, stoning, rejection, and thorns in the flesh. But Paul finished the race because he remembered Jesus.

E. H. Ijams was seventy-two when he began his last ministry at Highland Street Church of Christ in Memphis in 1958. Few men touched Highland Church in those days like Ijams. As time passed, his body failed him. Near the end, he spoke in a whisper, couldn't drive a car, and often ran out of energy. But he never quit. He never stopped.

Landon Saunders told me about a time he went to Memphis when Landon's ministry was under attack. In the midst of the uproar and quarreling, Landon was called to defend himself. Landon went to see Ijams before the meeting to seek advice and to ask Ijams to come to the meeting. Ijams said no. It was not his style to quarrel or dispute over words.

Saunders went to the meeting at a local hotel. He stood to defend himself before his accusers. As he walked to the podium, somebody opened the door at the back of the hall. Saunders could see out into the lobby. There was E. H. Ijams bowed in prayer.

When I think of the race we all must run, I think of Ijams: an old man at a meeting he didn't want to attend, in the lobby praying, trusting in the grace of God, remembering Jesus, and finishing the race.

In February 1978, my mother called to say my grandfather had died. I had stayed at his farm as a child. I remember he gave me horsey rides on his knee. So we packed our bags and made the six-hundred-mile trip to Pennsylvania. While there, local preacher Ray Beggs called. He had asked me to be part of his Wednesday night class when I was a teen. He taught me to memorize Scripture. He was the first to ask me to preach. He baptized me into Christ. Ray called to say he was sick with terrible stomach pains and asked me to preach the next day.

I was so torn. I was devastated by my grandfather's death. I hadn't brought any sermon notes. I felt like my family needed me. Ray understood. He preached the next day in the midst of pain.

A couple of weeks later, Ray learned he had a fast-acting cancer. It made me feel even worse that I had not taken his place. But Ray continued to preach. He never complained about the cancer. He never quit.

One of his lifelong goals was for his two preacher boys, Harve Smeltzer and me, to hold a gospel meeting for the church. The elders made the arrangements quickly. Harve did three nights. I did three nights. When we arrived for the meeting, Ray was back in the hospital and could not attend. Every night, he asked how the preaching went. The day the meeting finished, Ray Beggs passed away.

One of the last things he wrote was this: "I have cancer. I didn't want it. I didn't ask for it. I don't like it. But I'm not giving up."

He finished by the grace of God with his eyes fixed on Jesus.

Continuities. This volume on listening and making room is not a book on social work. It is not a political treatise. It describes a spiritual journey that may intersect with social work or political issues, but it is rooted in something else. We are reminded in 2 Timothy that the fundamental reason to listen and make room is our relationship with Jesus.

WHAT DO YOU THINK?

1. Talk about situations you know where somebody did not finish the race.

2. Share about a situation where somebody finished life strong.

3. Why do so many people who start to listen and begin to make room eventually quit?

4. What verse in 2 Timothy helps you the most?

5. Give your reaction to the stories about Ijams and Beggs.

6. Will you finish strong?

43

BE BOLD

GENESIS 18:1-14

The Second Chance Thrift Shop on North MacArthur Avenue in western Oklahoma City is operated by Delisa, a friend of ours. We attend church together. The store is a well-run operation selling used clothing, second-hand furniture, and knickknacks. On occasion, my wife, Sally, and others from church help Delisa with unpacking, sorting, and hanging the donated items. Recently, after Sally worked there one day, we heard alarming news. We just didn't know what to do.

Right before Sally joined Delisa and the others working at the store, a tall man came into the store, walked around, and then came up to the counter and pulled out a long knife. Fortunately, something happened, and he ran out. But it scared us.

It gave us a sense of feeling, "I don't know what to do." We wanted to help, but wondered if it was safe.

All of us have that reaction at times. Maybe it's national statistics about the recent rise in teenage suicide or the local increase in crime. We listen and then think, "I just don't know what to do about those things." Or maybe it's more localized. Some friends are headed for a divorce, and they ask us for help. As we search for a response, we realize we just don't know what to do. Or perhaps it's a vulnerable child we've tried to help. Suddenly, things get so complicated that we just don't know what to do. Or maybe I'm about ready to retire and don't have much money saved. As I look over the ledger, I conclude that I just don't know what to do.

So where do I find hope? How can I get a change in perspective? What can point me to effectiveness and success? Let me suggest a one-word answer. It may help us realign our thinking. It's a word often used in descriptions of God in the Bible.

It's the Hebrew word *pala'*. It's the word for "wonders." It means marvelous, surpassing, and extraordinary. It's also the word for "impossible." Pala' appears repeatedly to describe a God who does impossible things. He looks at one reality and imagines another.

In Genesis 18, Abraham and Sarah are pushing the century mark in age. They were told they would have children, but it doesn't look likely anymore. They were saying, "We just don't know what to do." Three angels came to announce that come springtime, Sarah would have a baby. Sarah overheard the conversation, looked at her old body, and started to laugh. But the angels didn't laugh. Instead they said, "Is anything too hard [pala'] for the LORD?" (Gen. 18:14). He looks at one reality and imagines another. He's the God of impossibilities.

In Exodus 15, Israel had been in slavery for four centuries. It was a clear case of "We don't know what to do." God sent Moses. He led them out of slavery and into a trap between the Red Sea on one side and Pharaoh's army on the other. Now Moses must have thought, "I don't know what to do." Then God split the sea. Moses sang a song in celebration. He sang, "Who is like you, O LORD, among the gods? Who is like you, majestic in holiness, terrible in glorious deeds, doing wonders?" (Exod. 15:11). He looks at one reality and imagines another. The word for "wonders" is pala'. He's the God of the impossible.

Psalm 78 might be called the psalm of impossibilities. It might also be called the psalm of forgetting. It's the story of how God did remarkable things and then Israel overlooked what God had accomplished. Verse 11 says, "They forgot what he had done, and the miracles [pala'] that he had shown them." He looks at one reality and imagines another. It's the God of pala'.

The same thing happened in Jeremiah 32. The Babylonians surrounded the city. The inhabitants are out of ammunition, out of food, out of water. The people were saying, "We don't know what to do." Jeremiah the prophet sat in prison. From his cell he writes, "Ah LORD God! It is you who made the heavens and the earth by your great power and by your outstretched arm. Nothing is too hard [pala'] for you" (Jer. 32:17). It's the God of pala'. He looks at one reality and imagines another.

An angel appeared to a virgin in Luke 1. He told her she would soon have a baby without a man. She must have given him that "I don't know what to do" look. The angel explained how it would happen. Then in verse 37, the angel said, "For with God nothing will be impossible." He looks at one reality and imagines another.

Jesus had just told a wealthy young man to give away his fortune in Matthew 19. The man couldn't do it. He must have thought, "I don't know what to do." People overhearing the conversation were equally confused. So, Jesus tried to explain by saying that rich people would have more difficulty going to heaven than a camel would crawling through the eye of a needle. Now they were more confused. They thought, "Who can go to heaven?" Jesus reminded them that with people it seems impossible, but with God all things are possible. He looks at one reality and imagines another.

God has always acted this way. So did Jesus. He looked out over the crowds. He saw their capital city streets lined with Roman crosses. They traveled from city to city under the gaze of foreign soldiers. The roads were dirt. Their floors were stone. Their clothing was rough. Their life expectancy was short. They had almost no medical care. Then he looked at those crowds and said, "I've come that you might have life and have it abundantly." He dreamed of the impossible. He looked at one reality and imagined another.

Theirs was a dog-eat-dog world, but Jesus said, "Do unto others as you would have them do unto you." It was a time when it was every man for himself. But Jesus said, "Be like me. I came not to be served but to serve." The world said that poor people didn't count. Jesus countered, "Be merciful, as your father in heaven is merciful." He looked at one reality and imagined another.

The God of pala' reminds us of who we serve. It calls us to look up, not in. It means we don't say, "It all depends on me," but we say, "It all depends upon him." It's not that I can't, but that God can.

History verifies all of this. A group of Christians who lived in the era of the Great Depression wondered what they could do about poverty. People were moving into Nashville to find work, but there were few jobs. A young man named E. H. Ijams and some others started the Nashville Central Church of Christ. Over the next twenty years, they helped hundreds of people find jobs. They averaged keeping 170 homeless people in their facilities every night. They preached the gospel every day of the week and had a free meal at noon every day. They did it for twenty years. During that time, they baptized about eight thousand people.[1]

A young Canadian boy graduated from Harding College in 1945. Someone had converted him out of a gang and told him to go to Harding. He did. When he finished school, he told the president, "I'm not sure what I'm supposed to do." President J. N. Armstrong said, "Go find somebody that needs the love of God and love them." Joe Cannon looked around the postwar world and thought the Japanese people needed to know about God's love. He went to Japan, and for about thirty years, he helped start more than three dozen congregations. Then he moved to Papua New Guinea, which was just emerging from the Stone Age, and started over a hundred congregations there.

I knew these men. Ijams mentored me. Cannon and I served on the same church staff. They were not millionaires or geniuses or corporate heads. But they believed in the God of pala' who could look at one reality and imagine another.

Delisa is one of those people. I mentioned her story earlier. Not long ago, a large man came into her thrift store and pulled out a long knife while Delisa was behind the counter. She came around and stood right in front of him. She's a small woman, but she looked up at his eyes and his knife. She told him, "I've been shot, cut, jailed, and raped. There's nothing you can do to me that hasn't already been done. What you need is Jesus. Put down that knife so we can pray."

She prayed for him. When she said Amen, he turned and left the store.

That is looking at one reality and imagining another.

---

[1] Read the whole story in Harold Shank, *It's All About God* (Nashville: 21st Century Christian, 2004), 121–33.

Continuities. When you listen, remember the God of pala'. When you try to find room, trust the God who looks at one reality and sees another.

WHAT DO YOU THINK?

1. The chapter refers to several passages where God does wonders or pala'. Which passage resonated the most with you?

2. How do these passages help us find hope in our sometimes hopeless world?

3. Knowing about the God of the impossible and about hope can reframe almost any situation. Discuss the implications of how such a worldview might be helpful in listening to the vulnerable and making room.

4. What seems impossible in your life or church right now? Spend time in prayer giving these situations to the God of pala'.

44

PRAYING FOR THE IMPOSSIBLE

ISAIAH 54:1-3

This is the story of three women and three children. One woman lived in Poland. The second one lived in Babylon. The third one lived in southern Palestine.

A few years ago, I visited Krakow, Poland. Our guide was a bitter woman with a chip on her shoulder. I couldn't figure out what was wrong. Then at one place on the tour, she stopped and blurted out her story.

She and her parents lived in Warsaw in 1939 when the Nazi army invaded Poland. Her father joined the Polish army, and in his absence, the Gestapo came to their apartment and pulled her mother and her two siblings out on the street. They wanted to know where her father was.

The mother screamed, "I don't know." They killed the four-year-old.

"Where is your husband?" "I don't know." They killed the two-year-old boy.

They beat her mother and left her on the street. During the 1944 Warsaw Uprising, her father came home. He and his wife had a couple of weeks together. Then the Gestapo returned and shot her father. Her mother was pregnant with our guide. In April, she gave birth. Her mother died that Christmas. Our guide was raised in an orphanage.

I can't get that woman out of my mind. Bitter. Frustrated with life. Living in the shadows with no hope. She built walls to keep others out.

A host of others know exactly how she felt. They know the bitterness and the frustration. They live in the shadows behind their self-built walls. They think, "There's nothing I can do. The world is wicked and there is no hope."

The second woman lived in Babylon during the forced exile of her people from Jerusalem. There seemed to be no hope. They lost the last war. Their king sat in a Babylonian prison. They were six hundred miles and seventy years from home. Weeds grew in their temple and sheep dung covered their prized public squares. It was a bitter, frustrating time living in the shadows behind those self-made walls.

Then Isaiah challenged her and the others to think a different way. God can turn your swords into plowshares, make you a light to the nations, and send you a servant to die for your sins. One of his most striking comments is about a mother and her child.

She's a bitter, frustrated woman living in the shadows behind walls she keeps intact. Isaiah says this to her:

> Sing, O barren one, who did not bear; break forth into singing
> and cry aloud, you who have not been in travail! For the chil-
> dren of the desolate one will be more than the children of her
> that is married, says the LORD. Enlarge the place of your tent,
> and let the curtains of your habitations be stretched out; hold
> not back, lengthen your cords and strengthen your stakes. For
> you will spread abroad to the right and to the left, and your
> descendants will possess the nations and will people the desolate
> cities. (Isa. 54:1–3)

The prophet tells the barren woman to sing happy songs. She should get ready for the midwife. Tell your husband to add on a room, buy a crib, for a baby is coming.

It's no surprise that when God looked to the future, he used a child. Adam and Eve were evicted from the Garden of Eden. The next verse is about a baby. Noah stepped off the ark into a desolate landscape. The next section has a list of children. Israel moaned under the slavery of Egypt. The

Israelite elders and wise men posed no threat to mighty Pharaoh. But the Hebrew women giving birth along the Nile brought the empire to its knees.

But Isaiah doesn't just speak about a child, he talks about a barren woman. They show up all through the Bible. Barren Sarah used by God to bless us all. Rachel the barren one becomes mother of thousands. Barren Hannah cries outside the tabernacle, but gives birth to Samuel, who becomes the prophet. Gabriel talks to a virgin teenager about a way to change the world, and barren Elizabeth and her child have front-row seats.

Isaiah told the people in the Babylonian ghetto that they would be saved by the child of a barren woman. Impossible! Babylon had an army. Babylon had money. Babylon had connections.

In the big picture, from our perspective over two thousand years later, we see what happened. The Babylonian army has not been a threat for twenty-five centuries. They have been bankrupt for millennia. But the children of the barren women continue to influence the entire world.

So Isaiah puts the question squarely before us. Are we like the woman in Krakow whose life overflows with hopelessness who said, "I can't" and "I won't"? Or are we like the barren woman in Babylon who orders in a crib and adds a room to the house?

The third woman was also barren. Sarah and Abraham didn't have children. They tried. In fact, Abraham tried to substitute his nephew Lot, his household servant Eliezer, and even slept with Sarah's maid, all to have a child. Then three angels visited in Genesis 18. One angel was God himself. They announced the baby's due date. Sarah laughed and laughed. The angels want to know why. Then comes the line in Genesis 18:14: "Is anything impossible for the LORD?"[1]

Early on, the Bible introduces a God who does the impossible. Because of him, barren Sarah becomes the mother of the faithful. Israel was enslaved in Egypt but was saved by the God who does the impossible. A whole nation was imprisoned in Babylon, and the God who did impossible things set them free. How can a teenage virgin give birth to the Son of God? Nothing is impossible with God!

---

[1] I am using my own translation of the Hebrew word often rendered "difficult," but here more appropriately as "impossible."

Isaiah was right. When life turns bitter, when events frustrate us, when we dare not step out of the shadows, and when we spend all our time building walls to keep people away, think of Isaiah.

Sing, O barren one. Order a crib. Add on a room. For the God who does impossible things is about to act!

Continuities.

- **Mission.** God created a good world. We broke it. He is on a mission to fix it. He challenges us to help him by listening to the vulnerable and making room for them.
- **Listening to Children.** The vulnerable, especially children, face lostness, loneliness, brokenness, sin, violence, and suffering. Jesus listened to children; so should we.
- **Listening to God about Children.** God blessed children because they were in his image and valuable to him. He counts on us to ensure children know they are important.
- **Making Room.** We change what's wrong because we are disciples. We serve others because he served us.
- **Hope.** Without hope we plan, but don't perform. When we put our trust in the one who can do the impossible and keep our eyes on Jesus, we find the hope to carry on.

WHAT DO YOU THINK?

1. Are you willing to listen to the voices of the world's most vulnerable people?

2. Are you willing to work with God and others to make room?

3. In what present situation do you need to listen, make room, and have hope?

4. For what impossible situations do you need to pray? Make a list and pray.

ORDER OF MESSAGE DELIVERY

The chapters in this book were originally presented to those who work in the sixty child care agencies associated with Churches of Christ. Their organization is called Network 1:27. Their website is http://network127.org/. The following table lists the title, the location, and the original date of those presentations. No conference was held in 2011.

Title	Location	Date
Would You Be Poured Out like Wine?	San Francisco, CA	1996
We've Come to the River	San Francisco, CA	1996
Birthright—Burden of the Past	Charleston, SC	1997
Blessing—Blueprint for the Future	Charleston, SC	1997
Praying for the Impossible	Little Rock, AR	1998
Engraving a Child's Heart	Little Rock, AR	1998
Everybody Wins	Louisville, KY	1999
Run with the Horses	Louisville, KY	1999
Courage to Be Different	Albuquerque, NM	2000
Practice Playing Second Fiddle	Albuquerque, NM	2000
How Can I Find Faith in All the Trouble I've Had?	Orlando, FL	2001
Why Each Child Is a Reason for Faith* (Listen and Make Room)	Orlando, FL	2001
How to Finish the Race	Tulsa, OK	2002
Alive to Growth—Evangelism Close to Home	Tulsa, OK	2002
Balancing Spiritual Portfolios	New York, NY	2003
Don't Cut Corners	New York, NY	2003

Mercy!	Ft. Worth, TX	2004
Life!	Ft. Worth, TX	2004
Let the Past Be the Past—at Last	Memphis, TN	2005
Lost in the City	Memphis, TN	2005
Calm in the Midst of the Storm	South Padre Island, TX	2006
Storm in the Midst of Calm	South Padre Island, TX	2006
If God Be for Us, Who Can Be against Us?	Chicago, IL	2007
Wind Changers	Chicago, IL	2007
A Time of Revival—the Jephthah Story	Kansas City, MO	2008
A Time for Renewal	Kansas City, MO	2008
Sing for Joy	Nashville, TN	2009
Wait for Me	Nashville, TN	2009
Listen to the Heartbeat	Oklahoma City, OK	2010
Our Father's Passion for the Hungry and Hurting	Oklahoma City, OK	2010
Refreshment	Atlanta, GA	2012
Ready	Atlanta, GA	2012
Danger Ahead—Unsafe for Children	Ft. Worth, TX	2013
The Dream Is Still Alive	Ft. Worth, TX	2013
Lift Your Hands and Get on Your Feet* (Don't Lose Sight of Jesus)	Cincinnati, OH	2014
Jesus Is the Best* (Wonderful, Wonderful, Jesus Is to Me)	Cincinnati, OH	2014
When a Child Asks	Searcy, AR	2015
Be Bold	Searcy, AR	2015
Now Is the Time to Speak Up	Huntsville, AL	2016
Now Dwells in You a Mighty Purpose	Huntsville, AL	2016
The Forgotten Creation* (It's Not Good Out There)	Abilene, TX	2017
Getting the Hearts of Our Children in the Right Place	Abilene, TX	2017
Preferred Route* (The Asked-for Child)	Bowling Green, KY	2018
Your Route Guidance Is Complete	Bowling Green, KY	2018
The Road to Sunday Morning Church	Bowling Green, KY	2018

* Indicates the message was retitled for *Listen and Make Room: Joining God in Welcoming Children.*

SELECTED BIBLIOGRAPHY

Anderson, Lynn. *They Smell Like Sheep*. West Monroe, LA: Howard Publishing Company, 1997.

Bailey, Kenneth E. *Poet & Peasant and Through Peasant Eyes*. Grand Rapids: Eerdmans, 1976.

Barrett, David. *Evangelize: A Historical Survey of the Concept*. Birmingham: New Hope, 1987.

Bennett, William J., John J. DiIulio Jr., and John Walters. *Body Count*. New York: Simon & Schuster, 1996.

Boggs, William. *Sin Boldly: But Trust God More Boldly Still*. Nashville: Abingdon Press, 1990.

Children's Defense Fund. *State of America's Children Yearbook 1996*. Washington, DC: CDF, 1996.

Covey, Stephen R. *The 7 Habits of Highly Effective People*. New York: Simon & Schuster, 1989.

Darr, Katheryn Pfisterer. *Isaiah's Vision and the Family of God*. Louisville: Westminster John Knox, 1994.

Dawkins, Richard. *The God Delusion*. Boston: Houghton Mifflin Harcourt, 2006.

Dawn, Marva. *In the Beginning*. Downers Grove, IL: InterVarsity Press, 2009.

Dickens, Charles. *The Life and Adventures of Martin Chuzzlewit*. London: Chapman & Hall, 1843.

Dikkers, Scott. *You Are Worthless*. Riverside, NJ: Andrews McMeel Publishing, 1999.

Exum, Jack. "The Story of the Loving Brother." *Image* (July/August 1993).

Farrar, Steve. *Finishing Strong: Going the Distance for Your Family*. Sisters, OR: Multnomah, 2000.

Faulkner, Paul. *Achieving Success without Failing Your Family: How 30 Successful Families Achieved Family Excellence*. West Monroe, LA: Howard Books, 1994.

Fifield, Adam. *A Mighty Purpose: How Jim Grant Sold the World on Saving Its Children*. New York: Other Press, 2015.

Fleisher, Mark S. *Beggars and Thieves: Lives of Urban Street Criminals*. Madison: University of Wisconsin Press, 1995.

Gergen, David. "A Bridge to Nowhere." *U.S. News & World Report* (September 9, 1996).

Greenspan, Bud. *Golden Moments in U.S. Olympic History*. Baarn, Netherlands: Polygram Video, 1996.

Harvey, Bonnie C. *D. L. Moody: The American Evangelist*. Uhrichsville, OH: Barbour & Company, 1997.

Hauerwas, Stanley, and William H. Willimon. *Resident Aliens*. Nashville: Abingdon, 1989.

Hemingway, Ernest. "The Capital of the World." In *The Complete Short Stories of Ernest Hemingway*. New York: Scribner, 1987.

Human Coalition. "American Casualties: Abortions in the U.S. Compared to World War II." Accessed February 21, 2019. https://www.humancoalition.org/graphics/american-casualties-abortions-us-compared-world-war-ii/.

Johnson, Luke Timothy. "Friendship with the World and Friendship with God: A Study of Discipleship in James." In *Brother of Jesus, Friend of God*. Grand Rapids: Eerdmans, 2004.

Kozol, Jonathan. *Amazing Grace*. New York: Perennial, 1995.

Lemaire, André. *Les écoles et la formation de la Bible dans l'ancien Israel*. Orbis biblicus et Orientalis, 39. Gottingen, Germany: Vandenshoeck und Ruprecht, 1981.

Leno, Jay. *Leading with My Chin*. New York: Harper Paperbacks, 1996.

Lewis, C. S. *Mere Christianity*. New York: Macmillan Publishing Company, 1977.

McCarthy, Patrick T. *2017 Kids Count Data Book*. Baltimore: Annie E. Casey Foundation, 2017.

McCarthy, Patrick T. *2018 Kids Count Data Book*. New York: Annie E. Casey Foundation, 2018.

Mercy Corps. "Quick Facts: What You Need to Know About Global Hunger." Accessed February 21, 2019. https://www.mercycorps.org/articles/quick-facts -what-you-need-know-about-global-hunger.

Mosier, Randy. "The Story of Hien Pham, as Told by Ravi Zacharias." *Tools for Christian Living* (blog). September 22, 2017. https://toolsforchristianliving .wordpress.com/2017/09/22/the-story-of-hien-pham-as-told-by-ravi -zacharias/.

Musurillo, Herbert Anthony. *The Acts of Christian Martyrs*. Oxford, UK: Oxford University Press, 1972.

North, Ira. "Benevolence." Eden Records. Nashville: Christian Publishing Company, 1966.

O'Connor, Stephen. *Orphan Trains*. Boston: Houghton Mifflin, 2001.

Peterson, Eugene. *Run with the Horses*. Downers Grove, IL: InterVarsity Press, 1983.

Roper, David H. "Praise, Poise, and Prayer." No. 3042. Palo Alto, CA: Peninsula Bible Church Discovery Publishing, 1972.

Sanford, Eva M., and William M. Green, trans. *Augustine: City of God*. Books 16–18.35. Loeb Classical Library. Cambridge, MA: Harvard University Press, 1965.

Schuller, Robert Harold. *The Be Happy Attitudes: Eight Positive Attitudes That Can Transform Your Life*. New York: World Books Publisher, 2002.

Shank, Harold. *It's All About God*. Nashville: 21st Century Christian, 2004.

Shelley, Marshall. "The Sightless, Wordless, Helpless Theologian." *Christianity Today* (April 26, 1993).

Shennan, Christopher. *The Making of a Personal Evangelist: Winning the World for Christ—One by One*. Morrisville, NC: Lulu Publishing, 2014.

Smedes, Lewis. *How Can It Be All Right When Everything Is All Wrong?* San Francisco: Harper and Row, 1982.

Wilburn, James R., ed. *Faith and Public Policy*. Lanham, MD: Lexington Books, 2002.

Wright, Christopher J. H. *Old Testament Ethics for the People of God*. Downers Grove, IL: IVP Academic, 2004.